ESSENTIAL
SPIRITUALITY

Gordon T. Smith

D1468683

OLIVER
NELSON

THOMAS NELSON PUBLISHERS
Nashville

To my parents
Cecil and Eunice Smith

Copyright © 1989, 1994 by Gordon T. Smith

All rights reserved. Written permission must be secured from the publisher to use or reproduce any part of this book, except for brief quotations in critical reviews or articles.

Published in Nashville, Tennessee, by Thomas Nelson, Inc., Publishers, and distributed in Canada by Word Communications, Ltd., Richmond, British Columbia.

First published in the Philippines by OMF Literature Inc., 776 Boni Avenue, Mandaluyong, Metro Manila.

The Bible version used in this publication is the New Revised Standard Version of the Bible. Copyright © 1989 by the Division of Christian Education of the National Council of the Churches of Christ in the United States of America. Scripture quotations marked NIV are taken from the HOLY BIBLE, NEW INTERNATIONAL VERSION®. Copyright © 1973, 1978, 1984 by International Bible Society. Used by permission of Zondervan Publishing House. All rights reserved.

Library of Congress Cataloging-in-Publication Data

Smith, Gordon T., 1953–
    Essential spirituality / Gordon T. Smith.
      p. cm.
    Originally published: Manila : OMF Literature, 1989.
    Includes bibliographical references.
    ISBN 0-7852-8343-9 (pbk.)
    1. Spiritual life—Christianity.   I. Title.
BV4501.2.S5328   1989
248—dc20   93-45037
                                     CIP

Printed in the United States of America.

1 2 3 4 5 6 — 99 98 97 96 95 94

Contents

Introduction

Essential Spirituality is primarily intended for men and women who want a deeper experience of the spiritual life. Great athletes are noted for their mastery of the fundamentals of their sport. Great soccer teams are those that have mastered the basics. Similarly, a deeper experience of the Christian life is consistently found in returning to the fundamentals. We need to ask basic questions again: What does it mean to be a Christian? What is Christian spirituality? What are the essential elements of a dynamic and growing life of faith? This work is intended as a guide for Christians who need some coaching in this return to spiritual fundamentals.

We will have one assumption throughout this study—that we are seeking to maximize the grace of God in our lives. We want to emphasize the possibilities of divine grace. We want to respond to the love of God and his call upon our lives thoroughly and vigorously. John Wesley found depth and vitality in his Christian experience in part because he was so revolted by the idea of being a half-Christian. He wanted to be everything that God wanted him to be; he wished to appropriate all of God's grace for him. A. W. Tozer suggested once that we are as spiritual as we wish to be—implying it is merely a matter of our willingness. There is much truth in this suggestion, and the experience of Wesley confirms that God willingly responds to the desire of sincere men and women who long to know him, know his grace in their lives, and serve him wholeheartedly.

But we need a guide. We need a working model that can help us see our lives as a whole and recognize the elements needed in our spirituality to assure a full and effective working of divine grace in our lives. This book responds to such a need by pointing to the classic disciplines and components of a Christian spirituality that have been consistently affirmed by each generation of Christians. We have much to learn from the saints who have preceded us. The following chapters bring together some of the accumulated wisdom of our spiritual forefathers and mothers.

The Christian life is a precious resource made possible by the grace of God. It is his merciful and wonderful gift. Jesus once identified this gift as living water (John 4:10, 13). His gift to thirsty men and women is living water so they will never thirst again. But Christians often forget that this gift has a property remarkably similar to the water we drink daily—it needs a container. Just as we cannot drink water unless it is contained in a pitcher or cup, so the living water of Jesus cannot be known unless it is contained—and the container is spiritual discipline.

To appreciate this, we must maintain a clear distinction between new life in Christ and our spirituality while recognizing the need for a spirituality. Imagine a tall pitcher full of cool, refreshing water. The gift of God is new life in Christ, which is analogous to the refreshing water. Spirituality and the spiritual disciplines are comparable to the pitcher or cup we use to quench our thirst. We can have neither water without a cup nor the living water without the disciplines of the Christian life. But the disciplines are not the Christian life; we must not confuse them.

When we drink cool, refreshing water, it would make no sense to complain that the cup from which we drink is hard and inflexible. We are thirsty, and the cup allows us to drink freely. It would be equally absurd to protest that the spiritual disciplines of the Christian life are hard and inflexible. They are the precious channels of the living water we seek. They are not ends in themselves, but without them there is no living water.

This reflective study is a call to spiritual discipline. And it is issued unapologetically. Be prepared for rigor, discipline, and perseverance. We seek living water, and we will know this water only when we return to the fundamental disciplines of Christian spirituality.

The study is divided into two parts. Part 1 addresses the nature of the Christian life and the need for a biblically and theologically sound spirituality, designed for the individual person, while also appropriating the spiritual wisdom of those who have gone ahead of us in the church. Part 2 delineates the five essential components of a Christian spirituality and provides some practical suggestions for their implementation. Throughout, I wish to respond to two crucial and basic questions: (1) What does it mean to be a Christian? and (2) What are the essential components of a Christian spirituality? We need to ask such questions as we seek renewal and strength in our spiritual pilgrimage.

PART ONE

Understanding Christian Spirituality

CHAPTER 1

Recovering Our Spiritual Heritage

*W*e need a model of spiritual life that is biblically and theologically sound and also one that appropriates the wisdom and spiritual insight of Christian tradition. The circumstances that face Christians approaching the twenty-first century are definitely unique. But if we are going to develop a mature spirituality, we need to appreciate how other Christians responded to their centuries and appropriated the grace of God for their unique situations. Our response will be different, but it will incorporate their wisdom and insight.

In other words, we need to recover our spiritual heritage. For Protestant Christians, this recovery needs to include a fresh awareness of many pre-Reformation spiritual traditions and those traditions found outside the confines of Protestant churches. The Protestant Reformation was a tremendous revival of biblical piety. But one of the negative effects of rejecting the Roman Catholic hierarchy was a break from many vital spiritual traditions that existed within the Roman communion.

Protestant Christians were thus cut off from the spiritual resources of a thousand years of Christian faith. Thankfully, contemporary Protestants are coming to an awareness of a spiritual treasury that includes but is not confined to the Reformation.[1]

CLASSIC MOTIFS FROM THE CHURCH'S SPIRITUAL HISTORY

One approach to the study of our spiritual heritage is to note the motifs of the Christian life that have captured the imaginations of Christians. In their appreciation, the contemporary Christian community can appropriate the wisdom of the church's spiritual directors.

Each period in church history was characterized by unique challenges and opportunities. The story of the church's two-thousand-year struggle with her own identity and with the societies in which she was established makes fascinating reading. It is possible to identify notable motifs that mirrored the spiritual ideal of distinct eras in the church's history. Though not unique to the periods with which I will identify them, these motifs idealized the spiritual life that captured Christian imagination within different spiritual traditions. There are many such motifs, but here I identify six that are particularly relevant to the contemporary church.[2]

The Desert

First, there is a sense in which the *desert* captured the spiritual ideals of Christians in the third and fourth centuries. The desert fathers uniquely embodied the spiritual aspirations of the church. Their willingness to forgo material comforts was linked to a commitment to discern and follow the will of God. That desire led them to abandon the comforts of civilized life. Instead, reacting against what they felt to be compromise with society in the church of their period, they chose to live in isolation and solitude, and they devoted themselves to prayer.[3] Included in their understanding of the Christian life was the conviction that the body is evil, that physical desires are wrong, and that the material or physical is detrimental to the spiritual. For them, a rejection of material comforts and self-denial, particularly of physical and sexual appetites, were synonymous with true spirituality.

And there were extremes. Simeon Stylites is famous for little else other than his thirty-seven-year stay on top of a stone column. But Christians of all generations and traditions recognize in Anthony (ca. 251–356) a spiritual master of great significance. His biography, attributed to the great theologian Athanasius, describes a man of simplicity, inner strength, and peace, with deep love for Christ and his fellow human beings. Anthony viewed his life as a direct response to the command of the Lord: "If you want to be perfect, go, sell your possessions and give to the poor, and you will have treasure in heaven." He sold all, retreating initially to a disused fort and eventually to a secluded mountain near the Red Sea. His spirituality was that of a hermit, but he had countless visitors who came for counsel and spiritual direction. His successors eventually formed small colonies of monks, precursors to monasteries.

Critical to the uniqueness and genius of Anthony and

the other desert fathers was their remarkable relationship with the desert itself. They recognized that the desert is an important biblical motif for encounter with God. The desert was significant in the life of Moses, the Israelites, the prophet Jeremiah, John the Baptist, and Jesus.

The desert was the sphere where spiritual sensitivity was most acute. It was a place of renewed commitment as the external comforts and nonessentials of life were cut away, as the emotional, physical, and spiritual crutches that sustain people were left behind. Consequently, it was a place where God could be met in an unprecedented manner. The desert fathers saw their flight to the desert as an encounter with their own identity that would refine their dependence on and commitment to God. They viewed it as a time of intense temptation and willingly faced up to the reality of sin and the evil one. But more, the desert represented for them an opportunity for a renewed awareness of God and his will. The desert, they believed, tears away personal masks and tests the authenticity of a Christian's faith.

Modern city-dwelling Christians would do well to recognize the value of the desert motif. The city breeds superficiality, and we need to retreat, possibly within the city itself, to a place of quiet, a place of few distractions. The noise of radios and traffic needs to be replaced by the stillness of God's presence. We are embodied souls, and there is a direct correlation between our inner space and the outer space. We need to find quiet.

It was in the desert that Anthony found the ingredient he considered essential to true spirituality—solitude. The quest for holiness was dependent, he believed, on personal solitude. For the desert fathers, solitude did not mean that a person was alone. Christians are never alone, for we are with God. In solitude, we can be silent before God, hear his voice, and be most keenly aware of divine mercy. The noise of the city and of a busy human community creates a spiritual distance for the soul from its Maker. We need silence before God to properly know God and discern his will. It is only as we learn solitude that we can confront the deep loneliness of our hearts and face up to secret sins and the darkness that lurk within us. There is no substitute for this baring of the soul before God.

Solitude, then, is a prerequisite for Christian community. Recent writers have appropriately stressed that the church is the body of Christ and thus should live in vibrant community. But this emphasis on community should never undermine the complementary call to being alone with God. We are reminded by the desert fathers that solitude is an essential dimension of an authentic spirituality. We need to return again and again to the desert and maintain a rhythm between silence and communication, between solitude and community.

The Monk

A second motif in church history is that of the *monk*. Monks and their monasteries tend to be regarded with disapproval by the average Protestant. They are often viewed as strange people who lived in ghettos with little religious and social impact. But this perception is false; it reflects a failure to listen as others of different ages in the history of the church tell their story.

Benedict of Nursia (480–547) was the founder of the monastic movement. Just as Anthony was appalled by the degenerate life of the city that was corrupting the spirituality of the church, Benedict fled urban life and set up small monastic communities—bands of men who could strive for holiness in community. He drew up a guide designed to govern this common life, which is known today as the Benedictine Rule. It encouraged simplicity and self-discipline.

The monks who joined Benedict were simple lay-people, peasants. The Rule directed them to live as a family with an abbot as father. Each monk was responsible not only for his own spiritual development but for that of his companions as well. The Rule provided for learning to enhance their devotional reading; then also it discouraged idleness by assuring routine and discipline. Most of all, Benedict sought to provide a guide for monks to live in the presence of God and eventually know the life of heaven.[4]

At least three dominant concerns reflected in the Rule are relevant to the twentieth-century Christian. First, the Rule affirmed a spirituality of community, on the conviction that spiritual growth toward maturity was to take place in community. That was not a denial of the value of solitude but a recognition that the hermit's life in itself was not an authentic spirituality.

Second, Benedict called for rhythm and balance in the routines of daily life. The daily life of the monk was remarkably ordinary. Rather than seek the miraculous and the spectacular, the monk was to delight in the mundane. His routine included both the passive and the active, from prayer, contemplation, meditation, and study of the Scriptures to such activities as work in the monastic gardens and fields, education, preaching, and works of charity. Our daily routines may have different components, but we can learn much of value from the order and simplicity of the monk's daily life.

Finally, the monastic movement was characterized by a profound and active concern for poor and underprivileged people. Neglected people of society throughout the Middle Ages found shelter, food, and medical care in the monasteries. That was particularly the case with the mendicant monastic orders, notably those founded by Dominic and Francis. They affirmed the principle that true spirituality cannot ignore the reality of poverty.

The Mystic

A third motif that played a major role in the spiritual history of the church is that of the *mystic*. Mysticism as a movement is found primarily, but not exclusively, during the late Middle Ages. Mysticism is difficult to define—but it can be understood best as a movement that encouraged a direct, personal, and experiential awareness of the presence of God. Arguably the high point of evangelical, biblical mysticism is found among the Spanish mystics, notably in Teresa of Avila (1515–82) and John of the Cross (1542–91).

As with the desert fathers and the rise of monasteries, Christian mysticism emerged as a protest against what was perceived to be a worldly church. There was an increasing concern that monasteries had become wealthy, and that a renewed call to poverty and spiritual community was justified. Mysticism was also, in part, a reaction to the imbalanced emphasis on rationalism in scholastic theology. The movement was an attempt to balance the intellectual with the affective, a union of the head (illumination of the mind) with the heart (affective love of God).

The mystics were convinced that a personal encounter with God is possible through prayer. They sought for a recovery of personal piety through a life of prayer, meditation, and contemplation. Mysticism became imbalanced when it led to a neglect of social concern or when it became so individualistic that it lost its moorings in the church. But in John and Teresa, we find a grand call to a spirituality that centered on affective prayer, the prayer of one who lived in intimate love with God. The intimate encounter with God was life transforming; in the relationship one could find abiding peace—a peace as intense as an inner light. In John, intimacy with God is never understood at the expense of God's character and transcendence. God is still the Holy One, and any degree of knowledge of God and peace in God is wholly of grace.

The mystics serve as a continual reminder to the twentieth-century Christian community that the experience of God is meant to be personal, dynamic, and intense. The Christian faith is not primarily an intellectual experience. It is very much a personal and intensely emotional commitment and relationship with a living God. Through the writings of the mystics, we are called to a life of prayer that features communion and contemplation as much as intercession.

The Called One

The fourth spiritual motif is associated with the Reformation, a period of the church's history that overlaps the height of mysticism. It is difficult to find a word or picture that best captures the spiritual revolution represented by Martin Luther (1483–1546) and John Calvin (1509–64). The ideal of a *called one* may depict it best.

The Reformers called for a spirituality that had three dominant features. First, it was founded on the principle of gratitude. The Protestant Reformers stressed that salvation was a free gift, and consequently, the Christian life was one of lived-out gratitude. They insisted that justification by faith alone was the heart of a true spirituality.

Second, the Reformers also recognized the transforming power of the holy Scriptures. They were ardent in their conviction that knowledge of the Word is pivotal to personal transformation in the image of Christ, and that a relationship with God is mediated by his Word.

Third, Luther and Calvin rejected the medieval distinction between the sacred and the secular. They believed that all Christians served God, regardless of their vocation, if they did so out of gratitude for their salvation and out of a sense of divine purpose. For Luther, the vocation of the preacher was not more sacred than that of the carpenter. Involvement in the world, through a vocation, was a sacred mandate for all God's children.

Protestant Christians today are still lagging behind in practice, if not in conviction, that all Christians receive a sacred call from God. Many still feel an emotional tug toward the idea that pastors and missionaries are somehow fulfilling a higher or more sacred vocation. An authentic spirituality must include the affirmation that all vocations have the potential to be a means by which God fulfills his kingdom purposes in the world. All Christians can be his kingdom agents within their vocations. The gathering of Christians for public worship, then, can be an opportunity for spiritual renewal and equipping for the diverse vocations to which members of the congregation have been called.

Thus, the called one delights in vocation out of gratitude to God and effectively fulfills that vocation in the world because of the transforming power of the Word.

The Pilgrim Soldier

The *pilgrim soldier* is a fifth important motif of the Christian life in the church's history. On the Protestant side, this perspective was probably best captured by the English Puritans (notably John Bunyan [1628–88], who authored *Pilgrim's Progress* and *The Holy War*). Among Catholics, we find it well exemplified by Ignatius Loyola (1491–1556) and Lorenzo Scupoli (1529–1610).

Scupoli published his "Spiritual Warfare" in 1589, and he captured the religious ideals of his age in building a spiritual tradition around the call of the apostle Paul to "put on the armor of God." With confidence in God, and in recognition of one's own inability, one could overcome the temptations of the evil one through spiritual exercises, prayer, and Communion. He recognized that true spirituality was of necessity marked by inner turmoil or "warfare." Spiritual maturity was possible only to the extent to which sin and temptation were confronted and routed.

Ignatius Loyola found the "consciousness examen" to be critical to ongoing conversion. We cannot be in union with Christ unless we are confronted with the reality of our sin and are able to turn from it.

The Puritans spoke of the "mortification of sin," a phrase that richly captures their conviction that there is no comfort until we are humbled by our sins. They believed that the conscience cannot be healed unless it is wounded, and therefore, a truly spiritual individual was well aware of personal sin.

But the pilgrim-soldier motif was not inwardly directed at the expense of outward activity. The soldier was also an ardent servant of Jesus Christ, and though the military motif has perhaps lost its contemporary appeal, we would do well to hear again the call to absolute obedience to the Lord of the heavens who wages continual warfare against the spiritual forces of darkness. We also need to recognize that all our actions bear continually upon this spiritual battle; we are either for Christ or against him in all that we say and do.

The Pietist

The sixth motif could be called that of the *pietist*—best exemplified by John Wesley and the revival he spearheaded in England in the eighteenth century. Wesley's spiritual heritage was a unique blend of Anglican spirituality, the church of which he was a member, his reading of the great mystics, and the influence of some Puritan forefathers. Those influences, together with his crisis in which he experienced divine grace, led to a movement that brought together many of the best elements of the different traditions. Wesley was convinced that it was intolerable to be anything less than a Christian who was actively seeking and actually experiencing personal and social holiness. He knew that God had something more for believers than merely providing them with an escape from judgment. God, for Wesley, was doing nothing less than making men and women new creations in Christ.

Wesley, therefore, ardently sought holiness. In his pastoral care for others, he established small groups or classes of Christians for the purpose of nurture and spiritual formation. The goal was holiness; the means was the appropriation of divine grace. But grace was available only as believers lived disciplined lives within Christian community. The Wesleyan revival dramatically altered the religious makeup of England as men and women, particularly poor ones, responded to Wesley's preaching and joined the classes.

A CONTEMPORARY MOTIF OF THE CHRISTIAN LIFE

James Houston has suggested that future generations may identify *the entrepreneur* as the motif of the twentieth century. Possibly no period in the history of the church has so stressed the potential of the church to accomplish great things for God while believing that we have the resources, methods, and techniques to do it.

The spirituality of this period tends to stress that all individuals have gifts and abilities of which they are stewards, just as all congregations have resources and opportunities to which they must respond. There is an enterprise to be accomplished, and Christians often feel they are duty bound to participate in and fulfill a mandate. Within this model of the Christian life, pastoral work and the oversight of the church are often judged in numerical terms. The role of the pastor is often perceived as that of one who administers programs.

This motif ably captures the spiritual principle, emphasized in many of the kingdom parables of Jesus, that Christians are stewards of the resources at their disposal, the abilities and talents given by God, and the opportunities for kingdom ministry that are before them. We are reminded that inherent in an authentic spirituality is participation in God's kingdom work in response to his call.

But there is a distinct danger in this perspective, particularly when viewed in isolation from other important aspects of what it means to be Christian. The entrepreneur model tends to view people in terms of productive capacities. It can easily become a secular perspective on people and work in that people are judged not for their inherent worth as children of God, created in his image, but for their ability to produce. Success and failure are so frequently determined according to purely numerical terms. Often the solution to an obstacle is defined as the application of a new method or technique. Many come to think of kingdom work as merely having the right strategy, as a matter of efficiency. The result is a model that has no biblical means for responding to failure, disappointment, and genuine obstacles to ministry.

There are elements of truth within this model of the spiritual life. But earnest Christians would do well to recognize the dangers and balance the ideals represented by this motif with those of other models that have been equally important in the church's history.

Here is a brief listing of some of the important truths about the spiritual life we can gather from reading the classics of the Christian spiritual heritage:

- A mature spiritual life requires both solitude and community, which means that true spirituality of necessity includes private prayer as well as identification with a community of believers within the church, in some expression or other.
- Spiritual growth most likely takes place in a context of routine and discipline.
- All believers are called to serve God, and they are called within a wide variety of vocations (a religious calling, or a calling to professional Christian ministry, is not a higher or superior vocation).
- Critical to growth in grace are the two character features of gratitude and humility.
- Spiritual warfare is both an inward and an outward battle, of ongoing inner conversion of turning from sin and an identification with God's kingdom activity in the world.
- Spiritual growth and vitality are directly linked to the appropriation of God's grace, which needs to include the study of Scripture, prayer, the life of the church and a community of believers, and some form of spiritual accountability.

This list is not meant to be exhaustive. But it does serve as a reminder of some of the critical factors that we need to consider as we develop a contemporary spirituality.

CHAPTER 2

A Tailor-Made Spirituality

ACKNOWLEDGING OUR DIFFERENCES

*T*rue Christianity is a living relationship with God, in Christ Jesus. This relationship is sacred; the living water that we have is a gift of God. But to sustain this gift, to abide in communion with God, and to grow in holiness, we need a spirituality that is designed to appropriate the grace of God, live in union with Christ, and serve him effectively. We need a mode of living that fulfills within us the ideals of the Christian life, including the inner grace of peace and joy as well as the outer grace of authentic vocation in the world and effective service for the Lord we love.

We need a spirituality that allows us to live in the world while not being cast in the world's mold. We need a spirituality that serves as a catalyst for vitality and growth. We also need a spirituality that integrates the different dimensions of the Christian life, the inner life of prayer and worship together with the outer life of service, the personal and the solitary with the corporate and communal. Finally, we need a spirituality that can handle the crises, challenges, and problems in our lives so that we can live with joy and peace despite difficulty, failure, and disappointment.

This is a tall order indeed. But we have the scriptural assurance that the grace of God is sufficient for whatever situation we might encounter. But to appropriate this grace, we need a spirituality that is specifically adapted to our age or personal maturity, personality type or temperament, gender, vocation or occupation, living situation, and cultural and social perspective. We need a tailor-made spirituality.

Teaching on spirituality often presumes that one model of the spiritual life is good for all. An individual, through personal experience, discovers that a specific approach to spirituality is particularly valuable. This is good. The danger, though, is that such an individual frequently becomes convinced that all good people should adopt an identical model. The person thinks that this model is the answer for virtually everyone and consequently embarks on a crusade to promote the merits of this approach. Naturally, it is not difficult to find a verse or scriptural text that supports the emphases of the proposed model. As a consequence, many people are helped. They, too, find that the approach is viable and effective—and promote the same pattern.

But the tragedy is that the model does not fit all people. Many are persuaded that the model preached is good, but they find they cannot live with it in peace. They feel guilty when they are not comfortable with the approach, and they often lead spiritual lives of deep frustration.

We urgently need to remember that not all Christians will have, or need to have, a similar spirituality. A wide variety of factors will shape a person's Christian life—both the inward relationship with God and the relationship with the world. I will examine them shortly. But for now it is important that we clearly understand this principle. Different people will have different spiritualities. This is liberating. It frees each Christian from the unrealistic expectations of others. But this principle is also sobering; it reminds us that we must avoid judging one another.

Nevertheless, the Scriptures and the accumulated wisdom of the Christian spiritual heritage affirm that despite the great diversity among Christians, essential components apply to all. They are few, but if we are to have a relevant and practical spirituality, we need to identify these essential components and creatively find ways to ensure that they are part of our spiritual lives.

The essential components of the spiritual life are like the ingredients in a recipe—every one of us needs to include them in our spiritual lives. But we will each have a different mix, a different arrangement, depending on at least six distinct factors: (1) age or personal maturity, (2) personality type or temperament, (3) gender, (4) vocation or occupation, (5) living situation, and (6) cultural and social perspective. We need a tailor-made spirituality. To do that, though, we need to make some measurements.

FACTORS AFFECTING A SPIRITUALITY

Age or Personal Maturity

One factor that definitely affects a spirituality is *age or personal maturity*. The contrast between a child and an adult is obvious. But we need to recognize more subtle developments. The transitions of life represent times of adjustment in our spiritual lives. Most analysts of moral and faith development see some standard transition points in adulthood. Ages and phases in a life cycle correspond to physical, mental, and emotional developments. Generally, adulthood is thought of in terms of three distinct phases—early adulthood, from the late teen years until the late thirties; mid-adulthood, from the late thirties until the early sixties; and later adulthood, from the early sixties onward.

These are not fixed times in a person's development, but they do represent phases that most people pass through in the journey of life. We normally recognize emotional immaturity in people who refuse to acknowledge that they are growing older. Conversely, we recognize maturity when people graciously and eagerly accept the transitions of life and adapt to them. Generally speaking, we need to recognize these transition times as opportunities to reflect on spirituality and respond to the new challenges and opportunities these transitions bring.

The early adult years of greater physical energy and exploration and opportunity need a spirituality that takes into account the needs of a young adult—choosing a vocation, choosing to marry or remain celibate, possibly raising a family, establishing life patterns, and so forth.

The mid-adult years usually represent a season of greater responsibility for the lives of others. These are often the peak years of productivity within a chosen vocation. In later adult years, a spirituality can draw upon the experience and wisdom that come with age. The seasons of life can represent transitions and changes that we joyfully accept or painfully struggle with. Acceptance of these transitions, and delight in the different seasons of life, is evidence of emotional and spiritual maturity. A sign of that acceptance is the maturity and development evident in spirituality.

Personality Type or Temperament

Another factor that affects a Christian spirituality is *personality type or temperament*. David Keirsey and Marilyn Bates in their fascinating study of temperament types, *Please Understand Me*,[1] effectively demonstrate what on the surface may seem obvious—people are different. Their point is that these differences are so fundamental, they will not change. Indeed, the point is that they do not need to change. That is the way people are. Keirsey and Bates argue that these differences are actually good, not bad. People think differently, respond to their world differently, perceive life differently, and have diverse ways of acting and responding. Their classification of these differences into sixteen classic types has given others the impetus to pursue their research into the field of spirituality. Is it not fair to suggest that differences in personal temperament will lead to differences in spirituality? Of course. If we seek to develop a spirituality that is tailor-made, it needs to match personality. We need to feel comfortable with it; it needs to fit us.

Gender

A third factor that for some may be equally important is that of *gender*. While it may be that we often overstate the differences, it is nevertheless true that men and women are not the same. They think, act, and respond in different, though it might be argued complementary, ways. Many categories by which we have classified male and female behavior are culturally conditioned and often fail to account for biblical expectations and priorities. It is absurd to suggest that a young boy has a feminine orientation because he plays with a dollhouse. That is a cultural perspective; the Scriptures may lead to a different conclusion. The idea that an aggressive girl is not feminine is equally questionable. The distinction between male and female is far more subtle. Further, the differences are not so absolute as some cultures tend to make them. It may well be that women tend to think in one way, but not absolutely, and that men tend to think in a different way. But when a man thinks in a way we might normally think a woman would respond, that does not make him less manly.

Let me suggest a perspective recognizing that the difference between men and women has some degree of continuity with physical differences. I would venture that generally men, in personal relationships, are more prone to take the initiative; women are more prone to respond. A woman most easily loves a man who has demonstrated his love for her; a man most easily loves when his initial expression of love is reciprocated. But this is not an absolute distinction, if indeed it actually exists. To respond in love is not the sole domain of women; initiative is not the sole domain of men. This would be only a tendency.

I might also note that the people of God, the church, are feminine toward God. We can affirm that the masculine language for God in the Scriptures is there not because God is male but because God is masculine toward humankind. Our love of God is in response to his love for us.

But the point here is simply this—that gender may be a factor in the development of a spirituality. Men and women are different. The recent emergence of literature that attempts to describe a feminine spirituality is, in part, a response to what is perceived to be a dominance of male-oriented literature in the church on the subject of spirituality.

Vocation or Occupation

Another factor that will certainly affect a spirituality is that of *vocation or occupation*. Is it not reasonable to conclude that the spirituality of a doctor and that of a mother at home with small children could be different? There will be some fundamental essentials in both spiritualities, but the visible expression will be different. The spirituality of an artist will be distinct from that of a politician. Much Roman Catholic spiritual literature has been written specifically for people with a religious vocation (i.e., priests and nuns). Yet more recent writings reflect a growing awareness of a spirituality designed expressly for people called to a nonreligious vocation.[2] This is a welcome development, and it points to a further need that individuals who share a vocation spend time in reflection on elements of an appropriate spirituality to sustain an individual within that vocation. God calls us. Then, in turn, that vocation becomes a factor in the shaping of a spirituality.

As we design a spirituality, we do so with the goal of seeking God's grace for our situations. In some vocations individuals need to recognize the existing stress factors and tensions unique to their vocation and assure that their spirituality is designed to respond adequately.

Living Situation

One's *living situation* will also be a factor in determining a spirituality. This may actually be one of the most critical factors, yet one that is easily overlooked. My search for the essential components to a spirituality came in response to a geographic transition in my life. After several years in a pastorate in Ontario, Canada, our family was transferred to Manila, Philippines. Initially, my primary activity was language study; later, my ministry focus was theological education. Through the various transitions, I realized that the outward expression of my spirituality would need to be different in Manila. If I failed to adapt to a new situation, I would not be able to appropriate the grace of God for that setting. Each geographic change entails inner stress, new temptations, and new difficulties. A spirituality needs to be so constructed as to respond appropriately.

But many times a spirituality takes for granted certain

structures and norms. For some, it may mean a style of worship or an intimate group of supportive Christians. For others, it may mean opportunities for service that are lost in the transition. Whatever the case, the point is that there are essential components to a spirituality, and a change in life setting requires that we reflect, within the new context, on how these components can be found in that setting.

Cultural and Social Perspective

Finally, *cultural and social perspective* will be a factor in a spirituality. Failure to recognize this often causes much misunderstanding and blocks a Christian community from developing a truly indigenous spiritual life. We have much to learn from one another across cultures. But in the end, we must give one another freedom within our cultural and social settings to develop a spirituality that is appropriate and dynamic. Spiritualities within different cultural and social situations may be remarkably different, or the differences may be quite small or subtle. Either way, this diversity is reflective of an authentic spirituality. Filipinos and Canadians will worship and pray, they will respond to God and appropriate his grace, in symbols, structures, and forms that are suitable to them.

RESPONDING TO GROWTH POINTS

Inevitable Change

Life is full of change, opportunities, and crises. Indeed, many people feel that life is overwhelming. They admit that they are unable to adjust to the constant flux of human life, particularly in contemporary urban society. Change is feared. New situations and challenges are seen as burdens rather than as invigorating opportunities. But change is as much a part of human life as current is to the life of a river. Learning to respond effectively to change is crucial to the development of a strong spirituality.

This challenge includes the acknowledgment of change in our lives. For example, I have met missionaries who, having lived in the midwestern United States, did not realize how different their lives would be after they had come to work in Manila, Philippines. The setting in both places was still urban, and for many, the religious subculture was similar, at least on the surface. But some of the important features of the missionary's previous life situation had vanished. Spiritual stress was the natural outcome of a failure to creatively respond to a new context. We need to begin by acknowledging changes in our lives if we want to adjust well.

Some changes we welcome eagerly perhaps, such as when we have an opportunity to leave home and go to a university or college, or when we get married and start a family, get a good job or change jobs, or move into a new neighborhood. In each case, we may very well welcome the transition in our lives. But there will be other times when we will not be so eager for the change—death of a spouse, close relative, or friend; the other person's transfer to another place because of work, study, or marriage; or loss of our employment. These changes are naturally undesirable. One could easily respond by rejecting the obvious results that these events bring to our lives. But essential to the development of a strong spirituality is the acceptance of ever-present changes in our lives and a creative response to new life circumstances, whether or not we welcome them.

More often than not, we will find that these changes in our lives open us to potential growth points. The human mind and heart are exceedingly complex. As the spirit of God performs divine surgery on our inner persons, transforming us into the image of God, he does so within (and through) our geographic and social contexts. Changes in our life settings unfold to reveal dimensions of our lives we were probably unaware of. New challenges create new tensions. New working relationships often reveal the different sides of character. Changes in our lives bring opportunities for growth because they usually uncover new sides of personality and commitment. A transition from living in a rural setting to a large city usually exposes a person to new temptations and challenges. Marriage, and the personal intimacy of this relationship, usually uncovers dimensions of our lives we were not forced to acknowledge before. A demanding or perhaps difficult work situation may force us to dig deeper than ever before into our inner spiritual resources granted by the grace of God.

The Need for Focus

Even if we do not experience external transitions and developments in our lives, it is still valuable for us to identify growth points and respond to them appropriately. In this respect it is helpful, through regular self-examination (which will be discussed more fully in chapter 7), to acknowledge areas in our lives that God would like to transform, and respond adequately and creatively. If I sense that the renewal of my mind is, at this time in my life, a priority for God, I will want to cultivate that dimension in my spirituality. If I sense that God is particularly concerned with my understanding and expression of my vocation in the world, it is appropriate to respond by developing this aspect of my life. If I grow in awareness, through the convicting work of the Spirit, to the needs of my marriage, it seems logical that I should adjust by giving special attention to my relationship with my wife.

Growth points. We cannot respond generally and vaguely to the promptings of the Spirit and to new opportunities and challenges that changes bring to our lives. Focus is needed. The human mind usually can deal only with one growth point at a time. We are not so formed that we can adequately respond to more than one sermon in a day, for example. Those who listen to several sermons on a Sunday, in public worship and on television, essentially choose to live on the surface, for they cannot effectively respond to that many sermons in one day. The human soul is far too complex. Therefore, through the promptings of the Spirit, through the ministry of the Word, and through our own meditation on Scripture and self-examination, we can unapologetically focus on a single growth point at a time and respond in our spirituality to that specific area of our lives. And our appreciation of the essential components of a Christian spirituality can help us design an appropriate response to a growth point.

The Need for Growth

We can also look at this from another angle. Not only do we need a spirituality that is an effective response to the growth points in our lives, we actually need a model of the spiritual life that fosters growth. Our natural inclination will be to live by a spirituality that makes us comfortable, affirms our choices and preferences, and will not disturb us. If growth in spiritual maturity—holiness—is our unqualified goal in the Christian life, out of necessity, we need a spiritual model that will stretch and challenge us continually. Often we need to be shaken out of our lethargy. We regularly need a sober encounter with the reality of sin. By stressing the need for a tailor-made spirituality, I am not saying that this spiritual model will always be comfortable and affirming. A true spirituality will consistently open us to growth, create opportunities for the voice of God to be heard, stretch us to full dependence on the grace of God for effective service, and regularly confront us with the reality of God's holiness and our sin.

The five essential components in a Christian life represent an essential spirituality for maximizing our growth potential. But spirituality cannot guarantee holiness in our spiritual experience. There is no model of a Christian spirituality that assures growth in holiness. Nevertheless, it can be inferred from our rich spiritual heritage that if certain key elements are found in an individual's life (and that of a Christian community), the person will have a consistently greater sensitivity to the work of God and a more effective response to his grace. We need a spirituality that inclines us toward growth in faith and fosters wisdom, discernment, obedience to the Word of God, service within the will of God, and love for the people of God. We need to develop a model, personally designed, that fosters spiritual growth and vitality.

CHAPTER 3

The Cross and Christian Discipleship

*I*f we discuss the factors that will shape individual spiritualities, the questions that we raise when we customize a spirituality, we must also consider what is foundational and basic to any Christian spirituality. Actually, the primary reference point in our spiritual growth will be the foundational questions of the Cross at the center and the mystical and earthly dimension of our experience. In this respect, we begin with the Cross.

Christian spirituality is the walk of faith in response to the act of Christ, which centers on his death on the cross, followed by his resurrection. The Cross becomes the central point in the history of the human race. More precisely, it becomes the single most important point of reference for the person who claims to love and serve the living God.

This walk of faith, in response to the Cross, is a coming home to the Father, the Creator, made possible by the work of Christ and effected within the believer by the

Spirit. It is not instantaneous. Believing on the Lord Jesus Christ does not bring automatic transformation. But it does bring a new orientation, a new perspective, a new life—a walk in a new direction. Christian spirituality is this new way, the way of faith in response to the Cross.

THE CENTRALITY OF THE CROSS

The crucial place of the Cross in history and therefore in the life of the Christian believer cannot be overstated. The Lamb who sits upon the throne of the universe is the Lamb who was slain. There is no other salvation except through the Crucified One. This reality becomes the dynamic center within the life of the believer. The centrality of the Cross is the most important theological principle in our understanding of the Christian life. Consequently, the cross is the central symbol of our faith.

The Cross proclaims that salvation is a gift. Believers have responded to an invitation to life, which in the Gospels is compared to an invitation to a banquet. We have not been chosen because of our merits, accomplishments, or faith. We have been chosen, invited, and called because of grace. Christ loved us while we yet hated him. He died for us even before we were born. Christian spirituality is, first and foremost, love of God and neighbor, yes, but it is love in response to the love of God. It is based on the simple conviction that we believe we are loved ones, loved by God.

Second, the Cross affirms that salvation is based on the forgiveness of sins. Believers are loved ones and, consequently, forgiven sinners. Christians believe in the forgiveness of sins. Sin is real for God. He cannot tolerate it; he cannot abide the presence of sin. Union with God, or salvation, is possible only if sin is accounted for—the price paid. There is no freedom, no salvation, unless sin is repented of, and forgiveness found and appropriated. Salvation depends on a knowledge of our forgiveness. And in God, forgiveness rests on this willingness—our willingness to repent and turn, to turn our backs on sin.

Third, the Cross declares that we are accepted unconditionally. We are loved, forgiven, and accepted—just as we are. Forgiveness is conditional—we must repent. But God's acceptance is unconditional—we are received, just as we are. We do not need to perform, achieve, or impress. The more we try to impress, the more our performance merely blinds us to God's love and the reality that we are accepted. Christian spirituality rests on this conviction. Spirituality is not ever an attempt to impress God or earn his love. It is, rather, the life of faith lived in assurance of divine acceptance.

Fourth, the Cross speaks of a new birth, a new order of existence. Christians, in becoming believers, are the same persons. We keep our names; we wear the same clothes; we eat the same food. But on another level, a dramatic and eternal change has been effected that affects the very core of our existence. In becoming believers, we have become new persons. We have, by the Spirit, been made right with God.

We might be tempted to overstate the reality of this change. Some speak or write of a change so thorough and effective that they are fully saved and no longer know the consequence of sin. Overstating the effects of believing in the Christ of the cross is not helpful. It is probably more accurate to recognize that each of us is fundamentally the same person after having believed. We are still sinners.

But this reality has been undermined! We are the same; yet we are different. In a fundamental and unsettling sense, the kingdom of light has launched a mission upon our dark hearts. We are the same people, but we have turned—we have turned to the light. The way of redemption may be long; our hearts were very dark. But we have turned, and in this sense, we can with confidence speak of ourselves as new people. We have been changed through the reality of faith in the Crucified One.

In each case, the various truths proclaimed by the Cross are appropriated by faith. By faith, we affirm that we are loved, forgiven, and accepted. It is by faith that we live as a new people. The evidence is not always there; in fact, the evidence may be rather slim that we are new people. But we believe. Not surprisingly, then, Christian spirituality is growth in faith. We are made God's people by a walk of faith; we know his life as we live in faith; we come to Christian maturity as we deepen the life of faith. This is the heart of Christian discipleship.

CHRISTIAN DISCIPLESHIP

The gospel of Matthew is the biblical introduction to, and handbook on, Christian discipleship. The abiding theme of this gospel is the reality of the lordship of Christ and new life found in being his disciple. A summary of these principles is found in chapter 4:

From that time Jesus began to proclaim, "Repent, for the kingdom of heaven has come near." As he walked by the Sea of Galilee, he saw two brothers, Simon, who is called Peter, and Andrew his brother, casting a net into the sea—for they were fishermen. And he said to them, "Follow me, and I will make you fish for people." Immediately they left their nets and followed him (vv. 17–20).

The meaning of discipleship is captured in the call of Jesus: "Follow me." Discipleship is a response to, and subsequent loyalty to, a person. Discipleship includes loyalty to a creed and a movement and possibly a congregation. But ultimately, its true meaning lies in loyalty to Jesus.

In choosing to follow Jesus, we submit. Discipleship is not cheap. There is a sense in which salvation is free—we cannot pay for or earn grace. Yet there is another sense in which it is costly. A few years ago a visiting evangelist to the city of Manila advertised for his mass gatherings with a slogan: "The price of admission is the same as the price of salvation—it's free." But is salvation that free? Does it actually cost us nothing? Though the gift of salvation is freely given, the New Testament message is that salvation is actually very costly. It will cost you your life. The disciples who followed Jesus left everything. In calling our fellow men and women to Christ, we must beware of misleading them. The call of Christ is to follow him, and in following, we leave our former lives behind. Full and authentic Christian spirituality is built on this principle.

This call to discipleship is a call to a new order of

existence—kingdom life. It is a call to know and live in the kingdom of God. It is a call to life! Jesus came proclaiming the kingdom—characterized as the kingdom of light and salvation, a kingdom ruled by the Lord of life. This new order of existence is patterned on a new value structure, a new purpose for living, and a new basis for seeking and knowing life. For Jesus, those who seek life will lose it; those who lose it for his sake will find it. Many who are last will be first; the meek, Jesus says, will inherit the earth.

This new order of life is both mystical and earthly. It is mystical in that a believer now lives in a personal relationship with the eternal Lord of the universe, who dwells in another dimension of life. It is earthly, for though the believer lives in union with God, the believer lives out Christian spirituality on earth.

Finally, the call of discipleship is a call to identify with the mission of Jesus. In imagery that was so meaningful to the first disciples, Jesus promised that he would make them fishers of people. The gospel of Matthew concludes with a mandate: Make disciples. The mission of Christ is more than just disciple making, but this is surely at the heart of his kingdom work—identifying with Jesus in the task of bringing men and women into a relationship of obedience, loyalty, and life, a new order of existence in the kingdom.

Someone may ask, "Is it possible to be a Christian and not be a disciple?" The answer is clear: A Christian is a disciple. That is what it means to be a Christian—to follow Christ as his disciple. Any teaching that bypasses this principle is not true to Scripture. Any teaching that fails to uphold the call to discipleship ultimately undermines the reality of the Cross, for the one who died rose again as Lord. The one who calls us to his banquet is the King. If we come, we submit. If we love, we obey. Christian spirituality is the walk of a disciple, in faith, in response to the call of Christ to lay down our lives.

HUMILITY AND GRATITUDE

Part 2 of this book will identify the five essential components of a Christian spirituality. But these components are meaningless apart from the two crucial attitudes of the believer—humility and gratitude. Growth in faith depends on growth in humility, on the one hand, and growth in gratitude, on the other. These are the marks of a spirituality rooted in the Cross.

An authentic spirituality ultimately depends not on what we do and what we have but on attitude. As the apostle Paul puts it in 1 Corinthians 8, knowledge merely puffs up; it has no value apart from love. Similarly, without *humility* and *gratitude*, a spirituality will merely puff up. It will not edify.

The concept of humility may be difficult to grasp, yet this grace is so vital to Christian experience that we must stretch our thinking and seek an understanding. Toward God, humility is an awareness of our creatureliness, our dependence on him as our Creator and Sustainer. But more, it is a growing recognition that we come before God empty-handed, as captured ably in the well-known hymn "Just as I Am." We have nothing with which to impress God or require him to bless us. We are creatures before a transcendent, holy God. We are sinners who know life only because we live under his mercy. Humility is simply living in the truth—recognizing the reality and character of God, and living in personal dependence on God as Creator and Savior.

But humility also has a social dimension in that it refers to self-perception within the human community. We rightly recognize the foolishness of arrogant people who think they are more clever than others. But Dag Hammarskjöld has noted that humility is just as much opposed to self-abasement as it is to self-exaltation. To be humble is to refuse to make comparisons.[1] Rather, in sober judgment of ourselves and of the task at hand, we are freed from the temptation to consider whether we are bigger or smaller, better or worse. We can engage the task we are called to do without the bondage of making comparisons. This means that we are now freed from the crushing blow of criticism and from the headiness of flattery. We still hear criticism and praise, but in humility we no longer fear the one and crave the other. We can accept both gracefully. Thus, Thomas Merton concludes that it is impossible to overestimate the value of true humility and its power in the Christian life.[2] In humility there is freedom—freedom from the desire for acknowledgment, praise, and vindication (the desire to be proven right).

The call to gratitude is one of the central exhortations of Scripture—a call to thanksgiving in all circumstances. Gratitude is a sign of humility; yet it is also the spiritual discipline that gives birth to and nurtures humility.

As a teenager, I was skeptical about religious faith. It

seemed to me that religion was a good thing, but that it should not be overdone. I thought that Christianity was true, but that it should be taken in small doses. One day, as we arrived home from a family holiday, my mother uttered a prayer as we drove into the driveway that was her expression on that kind of occasion: "Thank you, Lord, for a safe trip." Well, I decided it was time to state my case. I asked my mother why she thought we had some kind of special dispensation over our car when thousands had been on that road traveling safely. I wondered aloud why we should think that we had some kind of special treatment from God, and that for some reason God was caring particularly for us. I vividly remember her response: "Gordon, all of us travel under the mercy of God. The difference is that the Christian knows this, acknowledges it, and gives thanks." The difference, I now know, is one of living in the truth. And gratitude cannot be overdone.

In turning away from sin, we turn from a lack of gratitude to an attitude of thanksgiving. Then we can grow in our gratitude until it permeates every dimension of our lives. Indeed, there is a direct correspondence between the depth of our gratitude and the strength and vitality of our spiritual lives.

It is out of character for us to grumble, complain, or worry. Our deep need is to grow in joyful contentment. Without growth in gratitude, our spirituality will be crippled, and our task in the world will not bear fruit. Lack of gratitude is a sign of proud discontent, evidence that we think we deserve more. This ingratitude is pride, and it stifles life, joy, and peace.

In contrast, gratitude renews the human spirit and breathes life into our inward beings. However, we don't give thanks just because it is good for mental health. We give thanks because we recognize the goodness and mercy of God. These elements are found centrally in the reality of the Cross and the gift of life appropriated for us in Christ's death. In Christ—through nothing of ourselves—we have been chosen as God's children and have received his gift of life.

But there is more. In Christ, our eyes are opened to see the reality of God's grace in even the most difficult situation. The blinders have been removed from our eyes so we can now see a hand of mercy in the midst of the deepest wrong and recognize God's goodness in the midst of a predicament.

Notice the inherent distinction here. We do not give thanks *for* evil and difficult circumstances. Rather, our eyes have been opened to the reality of divine grace in the midst of difficulty, injustice, and even suffering. Consequently, gratitude reflects a decision to receive this grace of God—to see his mercy and goodness. Eventually, this way of seeing can become a habit of the heart—a hallmark of our lives. As such it will become central to our spirituality and our maturation as Christian believers. Both humility and gratitude are the personal attitudes that accompany and foster faith.

THE SUFFICIENCY OF GRACE

In Christ, all the fullness of the Deity dwells in bodily form. Consequently, all we need is found in him, and the

Scriptures affirm the sufficiency of Christ for believers in any situation. The key, though, is found in appropriating this grace.

In the Middle Ages, spirituality was often compared to a bridge.[3] Joseph de Guibert builds on this ancient image and notes that there are many varieties of bridges, with different styles and structures as well as different materials used to build them. Generally, the kind of bridge reflects the geological setting, the terrain on which the bridge must be built. But the style and form of the bridge also reflect the resources available to the builders. There are stone, wood, concrete, and steel bridges; there are simple straight bridges as well as grand suspension bridges over major canyons or rivers. The principle is simple: Different resources and different terrains require and allow for different kinds of bridges.

But materials cannot be combined at random. A wooden bridge cannot cross the Golden Gate in San Francisco; reinforced concrete cannot be mixed with wood. There must be consistency, or as de Guibert puts it, we need "an organic, balanced combination of materials and shapes." Similarly, we need to use modern materials, though we may well learn from ancient patterns and the craftsmanship of earlier bridge builders.

The bridge image has further application. We cannot transfer a particular bridge from one place to another. If we move to another place, we need a new bridge for a new context that appropriates the resources at hand. We need to adapt to different terrains. A spirituality needs to reflect two fundamental factors—the context in which we live, and the resources available to us. As we move from one place to another, or as there are transitions in our lives, we need to carefully study the new terrain and examine our resources. We need to reflect upon the kind of bridge that would be suitable for the new situation. We can learn from the experience of previous builders and even from our experience, but the bridge will be uniquely our own. We will incorporate the five essential components in a manner that is unique to the personal life situation, even though some of these components will overlap with those of others living in similar terrain.

Thus, in putting together a viable spirituality, the first principle is that your spirituality needs to uniquely fit your context and resources, and reflect an organic consistency. On the one hand, this should free you from feeling obligated or burdened by the spiritual pattern of your neighbor. One person's conscience and vision of the spiritual life may lead him up one path or across one bridge, but not everyone needs to follow him. On the other hand, this principle reminds you that you are responsible for your own spiritual walk. No one else can design it for you. Though there are friends and pastors and colleagues along the way, you ultimately need to resolve this matter for yourself.

Five essential components will be outlined in Part 2 of this book. They should ideally fit together into an organic whole in the life of the individual Christian. This book provides the ingredients, but you must decide how much of each ingredient needs to be included in your spirituality. A new Christian may feel the need to stress the renewal of the mind; another may see this segment of her life as needing extensive times of personal encounter with God; a third person may recognize the need for intense periods of spiritual direction. The point is this: You need to design a spirituality for yourself that adequately allows you to appropriate God's grace for spiritual growth and vitality in your present living and working situation.

God's grace is sufficient. We need to reaffirm this truth again and again. We have a tremendous promise within God's Word—that his grace is sufficient for whatever the situation. God will never give us a ravine that is too wide or deep for us to build a bridge across; further, he will always provide us with the needed resources.

We may get frustrated trying to find good books to read or despair we will not hear the Word of God preached effectively. We may feel very alone and think that a spiritual director is something we cannot possibly have. But we need to temper these feelings by an abiding conviction that though we may lack what we think we need, God has promised to be our provision. In response to this promise, we need to open our eyes with gratitude and make every effort to respond to what he does provide.

And we must appropriate his grace; we must live in conscious awareness of the means of grace that God has provided. Good books to read—we may need to pay a price. A faithful preacher of the Word—we may need to listen more carefully and willingly to the preacher God has provided. For a good spiritual director, we may need to travel and be near the person for several days. Again, there may be a price to pay. But we cannot presume upon God's grace. God will sustain us as we appropriate the means of grace that he provides.

CHAPTER 4

The Mystical Dimension of the Christian Life

WHAT DOES IT MEAN TO BE A CHRISTIAN?

*E*very sermon, each hour of public worship, every private prayer, assumes a basic understanding of the Christian life. Yet many believers, if asked directly, "What does it mean to be a Christian?" would hesitate and ponder and not be able to respond with clarity and confidence.

Many people have come to believe that the Christian life consists of a pattern of behavior. Ask people on the street corner and they will tell you that a Christian does some things and does not do other things. Talk to Christians themselves and they may tell you that there are three kinds of actions—those that Christians do, those that non-Christians do, and those in a neutral category that both Christians and non-Christians do. Quite apart from the question of whether such a division of activities is accurate, the view expressed is a flawed picture of what it means to be a Christian. Its focus, as we will see, is misplaced.

Others see the Christian life as a series of religious

duties distinct from nonreligious activities. These may include everything from the public act of worship to private prayers to dedicated service—but the Christian life, in their minds, still consists of these religious activities. Again, this view carries a misplaced focus.

The Christian life is fundamentally a relationship—a relationship with the living God. This concept cannot be overstated or stated too frequently. The Christian life is a relationship with the God of Abraham who has revealed himself in Jesus of Nazareth. Another understanding or expression of a spiritual life may have a religious dimension, but it cannot be identified as Christian. The Christian life is a relationship between the triune God and his people, the church, made possible by the death of Jesus on the cross.

We are going to tailor-make our spiritualities to our unique circumstances, to our personalities and temperaments, and to our vocational demands. But what must of necessity characterize every Christian spirituality is an intimate relationship with God.

THE CHALLENGE OF A MYSTICAL RELATIONSHIP

But this poses a problem. Our understanding of personal relationships has many dimensions. We have wife-husband, mother-child, teacher-student, colleague-colleague, and a wide variety of other relationships in our daily lives, including friendships that generally transcend these other levels of interpersonal involvement. It is probably easy for us to visualize these kinds of relationships in our minds. We can imagine the contexts and behavior patterns, and we can picture specific persons who have these relationships with us. But the most imaginative person would struggle to envision a relationship with someone we cannot see, hear, or touch. How do we maintain and nurture a relationship with a majestic, holy, and mysterious God?

This sounds like an absurd question to many Christians. They probably have lived with the reality of God as part of their common speech. God has always been there, and a relationship with this one named God is something they have never questioned. But think of it. Is it not amazing that common, sinful people can enjoy a relationship of joy, love, and even collegiality (did he not call us coworkers?) with the God who made the heavens and the earth? We cannot take it for granted.

Our relationship with God cannot be presumed upon, on account of our creatureliness and our sin. Further, modern urban life is not conducive to the spiritual life. Often our casual assumption of God's accessibility and availability is a sign that our relationship with him lacks vitality and depth. We must recognize that this relationship crosses two spheres of existence, between nature and supranature. It is a mystical relationship in that it transcends the material world.

It is astonishing that the living God actually seeks those who would worship him in spirit and in truth. This same God invites us to his banqueting table. Our Creator welcomes all who are hungry and thirsty, and who willingly respond to the emptiness in their hearts with a rejection of sin and a trust in the only one who can fill the void. But the relationship is still a mystical one, demand-ing care, thoughtfulness, and spiritual discipline if it is to be sustained and strengthened. In the goodness of God, we have a wealth of resources—the words of Scripture and the devotional writings from the church's history. We are not alone in our quest.

NEW TESTAMENT IMAGES OF THE CHRISTIAN LIFE

How are we to understand and sustain the Christian life? Through the Scriptures, God has provided a variety of images or pictures to help us understand who he is and how we can know, love, and serve him. And in examining our Christian heritage, we can discern how our spiritual forefathers and mothers were able to main-tain a relationship with the God of the Bible. (Chapter 1 emphasized the need to recover that spiritual heritage.) We are not the first to attempt what may seem over-whelming—a personal relationship with the Creator God.

The Bible helps us to understand what it means to be a Christian through picture language. Hundreds of images, taken from all dimensions of human life, serve as win-dows into the reality of God and what it means to be in a relationship with him. Three of these images, I believe, are central to the New Testament, particularly in the epistles of Paul and the writings of John. They portray the mystical dimension of the Christian life.

The Child

First, this life is pictured as that of *a child*. The believer is portrayed as a child of the heavenly Father. In his epistle to the Galatians, Paul writes,

> For in Christ Jesus you are all children of God through faith (3:26).

> But when the fullness of time had come, God sent his Son, born of a woman, born under the law, in order to redeem those who were under the law, so that we might receive adoption as children. And because you are children, God has sent the Spirit of his Son into our hearts, crying, "Abba! Father!" So you are no longer a slave but a child, and if a child then also an heir, through God (4:4–7).

Christ came specifically so that we, as orphaned men and women, might become children of the Father. That was the mission of God, his very purpose in revealing himself through the incarnate Christ.

This image of the Christian life is important to the New Testament writers. John's gospel assumes the doctrine of the Fatherhood of God, and it emphasizes constantly the intimate relationship of Jesus with his Father. The unique Sonship of Jesus is the model for the maturing (redeemed) childlikeness that we enter by becoming disciples of Jesus. Through his death, Jesus makes it possible for us to be children of the Father, and in his life he exhibits what that relationship means.

We are children of our Father by virtue of the indwelling Spirit. It is by the Spirit that we have an inner assurance of our identity as children of the Father, and it is by the Spirit that we can know our Father intimately and maintain a relationship of love with him.

Though the Christian life is fundamentally a mystical relationship with God, it also has a visible dimension that is unavoidably linked to it—the relationship of the believer with spiritual brothers and sisters. John emphasizes in his first epistle that love of God is conceivable only when there is a corresponding love for fellow believers. He joyfully declares, "See what love the Father has given us, that we should be called children of God" (1 John 3:1). But then he is very blunt:

> "Those who say, 'I love God,' and hate their brothers or sisters, are liars; for those who do not love a brother or sister whom they have seen, cannot love God whom they have not seen. The commandment we have from him is this: those who love God must love their brothers and sisters also" (1 John 4:20–21).

The close interdependence between a relationship with God and a relationship with fellow believers will be a constant theme of this book. Though distinct, these two dimensions of the Christian life are inseparable and mutually dependent: the solitary and the communal, the love of God and the love of brothers and sisters, the mystical and the earthly.

The child as an image of the spiritual life is one that has been rediscovered in recent years by theologians. James Houston suggests that this image of the Christian life is particularly appropriate for the contemporary Christian in the face of secular humanism, urbanization, and the stress on technological, self-confident humanity.[1] This image provides a profound sense of identity, for which modern people cry out. It acknowledges that as children, we are dependent learners, and it affirms the principle of loyalty in a pluralistic and rapidly changing society. Houston suggests that for many people, the image of spiritual children will significantly enhance their comprehension of a Christian's relationship with God.

Union with Christ

Second, the Christian life is pictured as *union with Christ*. Believers are portrayed as ones who live in a unique bond of fellowship with the ascended Lord Jesus. Our baptism, initiating us as Christian believers, symbolizes our union with Christ in his death and resurrection (Rom. 6:3–4). Paul speaks of this image in the epistle to the Colossians:

"As you therefore have received Christ Jesus the Lord, continue to live your lives in him, rooted and built up in him and established in the faith, just as you were taught, abounding in thanksgiving" (2:6–7).

Though the apostle goes on to stress other critical aspects of the Christian life, this constitutes a simple statement of what that life is. In coming to Christian faith, we entered into a relationship with Jesus. Now, as we grow and mature in our faith, we do not move beyond that fundamental principle—the relationship with Jesus. Our commitment is to deepen and strengthen that bond.

John's gospel provides the most graphic New Testament example of this image in the well-known passage describing the vine and the branches. In the words of Jesus,

> "Abide in me as I abide in you. Just as the branch cannot bear fruit by itself unless it abides in the vine, neither can you unless you abide in me. I am the vine, you are the branches" (15:4–5).

Here the mystical relationship of believers with their Lord is depicted as vine gardening. Spiritual life in a natural, material world is somehow, in ways we can hardly comprehend, a mystical union with the ascended Lord Jesus. We can literally live in union with Christ. He is the source of life—our emotional, spiritual, intellectual, and even physical energy. This relationship confounds the materialist, for the Christian actually sees this mystical union with Christ to be the central fact of existence.

Yet we need to go a step further. The expression "union with Christ" still needs to be explained in practical terms. What does it mean not in abstract or theological language but in everyday life to be in union with an ascended Lord? This formula may be helpful: True spirituality is knowing, loving, and serving Jesus.[2] Though a summary statement like this cannot capture in full what it means to be in union with Christ, it is useful as we look for ways in which to structure a spiritual life. We seek to know Jesus of Nazareth intimately. We seek to love him ardently. We seek to serve him wholeheartedly and effectively.

In following this formula, we avoid serving someone we do not love or loving someone we do not know. Service without love is dry and legalistic and eventually will lack any measure of compassion. Love without knowledge is sentimentalism. Rather, as Christians, our longing is to know Jesus, who reveals fully the God of heaven; our desire is to love him in response to his love for us; our commitment is to serve him and to do so effectively.

There is a certain logical progression here—we serve the one we love, the one we have come to know. Knowledge precedes love, which in turn precedes service. But it is not so simple. Actually, each of these dimensions informs and strengthens the other. Service for Christ deepens our knowledge and strengthens our love. Love frees our minds to know him better. The three are interdependent, forming an integrated spirituality. Together they form one way of understanding what it means to be in union with Christ.

Just as the first image of being spiritual children included the horizontal dimension of love of brothers and sisters, union with Christ cannot be solitary. Union with Christ of necessity means union with his body, the church. True spirituality, consequently, must be conceived in both personal and corporate forms. It includes community—not the community of a social club, but the community of a living, organic body of believers, worshiping and serving one Head, Jesus Christ. Union with Christ includes a dynamic relationship with God's people.

Walking in the Spirit

A third image of the Christian life portrayed in the New Testament is that of *walking in the Spirit*. We are children of the Father, for we have the Spirit present within us. It is by the Spirit that we cry out "Abba! Father!" inwardly assured of his love and care. We are united with Christ through the ministry of the Holy Spirit, for it is by the Spirit that we are born again to new life. We cannot ignore the truth that the Spirit is vital to the other New Testament images. Nevertheless, there is a distinct and important New Testament image that pictures the believer in a special relationship with the Spirit.

In Galatians 3:1–3, Paul asserts that Christians received the Spirit by believing what was heard, not by observing the law. The apostle then expresses amazement that anyone who came to faith in such a manner would attempt to reach the goal of spiritual maturity through human effort. Can this be done? His reply is an emphatic "No!" Human effort cannot maintain the Christian life and assure its maturation. In other words, Paul is warning the early Christians against the temptation of living the Christian life through willpower—the will to obey the law.

Though obedience is vital to the Christian experience, freedom from sin is possible only in submission to the Holy Spirit. We are all well aware of the frustrations of trying to live the Christian life. The road, as we look back, seems marked by constant failure. We are battered and bruised by our daily struggle with sin. Paul describes his wrestling with sin in chapter 7 of his epistle to the Romans. He understood, and he knew the solution. He calls us to walk in the Spirit: "Live by the Spirit, I say, and do not gratify the desires of the flesh. . . . If we live by the Spirit, let us also be guided by the Spirit" (Gal. 5:16, 25).

In the following chapters, I will attempt to identify the elements of a full Christian spirituality. Each of these elements is provided by God to foster spiritual growth toward maturity, which includes freedom from the habit of sin. There is no renewal in our lives without growth in holiness and victory over sin. But no structure or component of the spiritual life will, in itself, free us from sin. The component may be good and necessary. Ultimately, however, freedom from sin is possible only through submission to the Spirit who bears the fruit of the Spirit within us.

Finally, it is worth noting that this image, like the other two, also includes the matter of our relationship with fellow believers. Fullness of the Spirit leads to mutual submission (Eph. 5:18, 21); freedom in the Spirit is freedom to serve one another in love (Gal. 5:13).

These three images of the spiritual life—spiritual children, union with Christ, and walking in the Spirit—are not three distinct relationships. Each image links the Christian with a person of the holy Trinity—Father, Son, and Spirit, respectively. But this does not imply that there are three kinds of relationships, or that there is a different relationship with each member of the Trinity. Rather, our relationship with God is one. We are in fellowship with God, through Christ, by means of the inner work of the Spirit. The images in the New Testament are merely different ways of viewing this central truth: That by virtue of the saving work of God in Christ, we can enter into a personal relationship with him. We are children of the Father only by the Spirit. Similarly, union with Christ and walking in the Spirit are different ways of viewing the same reality.

This is most evident in the epistle to the Romans where Paul unites and blends all three images in a grand description of the Christian life. Notice how the three images are woven together into a tapestry:

> But you are not in the flesh; you are in the Spirit, since the Spirit of God dwells in you. Anyone who does not have the Spirit of Christ does not belong to him. But if Christ is in you, though the body is dead because of sin, the Spirit is life because of righteousness. If the Spirit of him who raised Jesus from the dead dwells in you, he who raised Christ from the dead will give life to your mortal bodies also through his Spirit that dwells in you. . . . For if you live according to the flesh, you will die; but if by the Spirit you put to death the deeds of the body, you will live. For all who are led by the Spirit of God are children of God. For you did not receive a spirit of slavery to fall back into fear, but you have received a spirit of adoption (Rom. 8:9–11, 13–16).

The value of recognizing the different images is that each can reveal a distinct dimension of our relationship with God. Aspects of our relationship, expressed in varied images, may capture our imaginations and foster periods of spiritual growth. It is helpful to allow one of these images to be the source of inspiration and the focus of meditation at different points in our lives while recognizing that in time we want to appreciate all images found in the New Testament. Each casts a different light on the rich and varied aspects of a relationship with the living God.

Do not hesitate to allow one of these images to spark your imagination and be the focus of your thoughts as you read the next chapters of this book. Maintaining that image in your mind can preserve a healthy understanding of the Christian life as we work through the question of spiritual discipline. The sole purpose of spiritual discipline is to nurture the relationship with God.

PRAYER AND SPIRITUAL TRANSFORMATION

There are two implications of the reality that the Christian life has a mystical dimension—the habit of prayer and the commitment to spiritual transformation.

Prayer

Prayer is the single most convincing evidence that the Christian life has a mystical dimension. The life of prayer is a continual reflection of a conviction that there is more to life than what is visible. Prayer speaks of another reality—and for the Christian, that reality is God. The Christian life is mystical in that it is lived in terms of two realities—the visible world and God. The Christian believes not only that God exists but that he lives in fellowship with his creation. And the chief means of fellowship is prayer. Further, the Christian lives with the conviction that God answers prayer—that prayer makes a difference. Prayer is not just words; it is personal communion with the Creator-Redeemer. It is heartfelt expression of real need to one who is capable of understanding and responding with wisdom and strength.

Not all prayer is good or true prayer. There are two simple criteria of authentic prayer: faith and humility. The Scriptures affirm that true prayer is prayer in confidence in the fact that Jesus is the ascended Lord, capable of understanding our needs and responding with wisdom and power (Heb. 4:14–16). But faith without humility is presumption. Prayer is the cry of a dependent child on a heavenly Father. True prayer no longer seeks to impress or gets caught up with the temptation to manipulate with words (Matt. 6:5–8). True prayer arises from a heart that has forgiven as it knows the forgiveness of God (Matt. 6:14–15). That is, true prayer is characterized by humility as well as faith.

The prayer of faith and humility is at the heart of the Christian life. Growth in our spiritual experience depends on growth in our life of prayer; spiritual direction, as we shall see, includes various elements, but the focus is on prayer. Prayer is at the heart of spiritual experience because the Christian life is mystical—a life lived in communion with and dependence on God.

Spiritual Transformation

The second evidence of the mystical dimension of the Christian life is the reality of spiritual transformation. That is, through our encounter with God in Christ of Calvary, our lives are changed. A true spirituality will lead to a deepening of the relationship with God, which will lead to spiritual maturity in Christ.

A relationship with God is never static; it is dynamic. It will lead to growth in holiness. God's unqualified purpose for men and women in relationship with him is that they be transformed according to his image.

And God is a holy God. He is truly interested in salvation; his purposes are to redeem men and women. But he redeems in order to form a holy people, a people called by his name. Any spiritual tradition that downplays the biblical call to personal and corporate holiness is not faithful to the biblical message. Holiness is not optional for someone who claims to be a child of God. If a spirituality is tailor-made, we can readily see it as right in that it fosters and assures growth in holiness. A relationship with God cannot be strengthened unless we are prepared to turn from sin, long for the righteousness of God, and allow the Spirit to transform us into God's image.

Spiritual transformation can be compared to the experience of becoming a mature child. Through regeneration, we are newcomers to the faith, feeding on spiritual milk. But as we walk in the faith, we mature in grace, learning to feed on more substantial spiritual food. Each growth point along the way is actually a further refining of our character in accordance with the holy character of God. Toleration of sin in our lives is as absurd as a doctor's toleration of sickness. It is rejection of life and of God. And this, for me, is one of the most helpful ways of thinking about holiness—as the full expression of health and life.

It will take a long time before I forget my first two years in the Philippines. When my family moved there, we were involved in language study, and then I became an instructor in theology at a seminary in Manila. But what was most noteworthy of those initial years was that we became very acquainted with the local hospitals for the simple reason that on average once a month, a member of our family was admitted for some reason or another. One of my sons had a serious allergic reaction that made it very difficult for him to breathe, and he had to be taken regularly to the emergency department. My wife at one point had hepatitis and then later the dreaded dengue fever. I had typhoid fever that left me in bed for more than a week.

I remember once sitting in the waiting room of one of the hospitals when my wife had hepatitis. As I sat there, I was struck by a fundamental longing from the depth of my being for health and strength. I longed for it for myself; I longed for it for my family. Nothing else seemed to matter—it was the dominant concern of my life. I was weary of sickness, of the hospital, of doctors, even though they were well-intentioned.

And when my wife was well and back at home, I recalled that feeling, that longing for health, and recognized that holiness is nothing more than thorough and radical wholeness—wherein our entire beings are healthy, right, and true. I saw that if we had eyes to see and ears to hear, we would recognize that we are sick, and we would seek holiness because we long for health and life. We would see that sin is sickness and death; holiness is life. And it would be evident that we live to the degree that we seek and know the holiness of God. Our desire for a vital spirituality is essentially a longing for God and for wholeness in God. The hunger for spiritual maturity is a longing for life.

The biblical ideal of holiness is summarized in the Old and New Testaments as love of God and neighbor. The purpose of a Christian spirituality is ultimately to foster love in both spheres. The Christian life is mystical in that God by his grace does sustain our lives and transform us. We are not merely awaiting some future transformation, but by God's grace, we are growing in holiness even now. Even now, we can know a substantial measure of freedom from sin; even now, we can know the transforming grace of God renewing and invigorating our lives.

CHAPTER 5

The Earthly Dimension of the Christian Life

THE CHRISTIAN AND THE WORLD

*W*hat does it mean to be a Christian? Chapter 4 stressed that the Christian life is a mystical relationship with the holy Trinity. But this perspective represents only one dimension of what it means to be a Christian. Although it answers the question in terms of the supernatural, this view does not give us much insight into what the Christian life means in terms of the natural—the created order. For that we need to turn to another New Testament image—the kingdom of God.

As we develop a viable spirituality that will enable us to know the grace of God, we will see that a true spiritual model must account for the fact that we live in a real, concrete, tangible world. True spirituality is not otherworldly; rather, it enables us to be fully in the world. Jesus himself, in his prayer recorded in John 17, explicitly says that he is not asking that we be taken out of the world. His prayer, instead, is that we would be made holy in the world—in but not of the world. All authentic

61

models of spirituality will, then, take this dimension into account.

The Christian life is lived under the kingdom rule of God. This recognition is essential if we are to fully appreciate our relationship to the world and understand what it means to fulfill our vocations within diverse social contexts.

The incarnation of Christ gloriously affirms that the Christian life is mystical, but it also declares that true spirituality is an earthly reality. It is a life lived as a citizen of this world. This conviction arises in part from a knowledge that the world is created by God, and that his redemption takes place in space and time, in the created order.

But this can be confusing. We recognize that we are of this world, but we also see clearly that our identity as Christians is far removed from the values of contemporary society. We know that we are citizens of this world, but we are also convinced that our home is with the Father in heaven. Even as the New Testament graciously provides us with images so that we can appreciate the mystical dimension of the Christian life, it provides us with a central image that captures the meaning of the earthly dimension of our spiritual existence. We find it principally, but not exclusively, in the announcement and teaching of Jesus concerning the kingdom of God. But to appreciate the significance of Jesus' announcement, we need to see the bigger picture.

THE KINGDOM AND THE CHRISTIAN

The Scriptures emphasize that the eternal plan of God is to bring about the reconciliation of all things. This divine purpose is identified as the kingdom or reign of God. God's purpose is to establish his kingdom in and through human history. If King David's kingdom is a foretaste of this divine kingdom, Jesus Christ represents the true and eternal King. Consequently, the kingdom is found in Jesus Christ as embodied in his presence and his rule. To live in the kingdom of God is to come under the salvation and authority of Jesus of Nazareth. Jesus came announcing the kingdom. His evangelism was to announce the fulfillment of the kingdom in himself and invite men and women to repent and live under his kingdom rule. Hence, to be a Christian is to live under the dynamic rule of Christ.

But there is more to this. Jesus, in announcing the presence of the kingdom, clearly implies that his kingdom is not merely a matter of individual responses to his invitation. He is proclaiming his messianic identity and right to rule over all things—over the whole created order.

Paul affirms that the mission of God in Christ is not merely to redeem a few individuals here and there but to reconcile all things in heaven and on earth to himself. But this reconciliation is possible only insofar as Christ is Lord. All things must be subjected to him. In the writings of Paul we read,

> He [God] has made known to us the mystery of his will, according to his good pleasure that he set forth in

Christ, as a plan for the fullness of time, to gather up all
things in him, things in heaven and things on earth
(Eph. 1:9–10).

For in him all the fullness of God was pleased to dwell,
and through him God was pleased to reconcile to
himself all things, whether on earth or in heaven, by
making peace through the blood of his cross (Col.
1:19–20).

This is tremendous news! It is exhilarating to think that
in and through Christ Jesus, God is bringing peace between himself and the whole created order. It is no wonder, then, that we read in chapter 8 of Paul's epistle to the
Romans that the whole creation is groaning in anticipation of our full redemption as the children of God.

We need, though, to add a cautionary but critical note.
The kingdom is fulfilled, but it is not yet consummated.
The King has come and has announced the kingdom, and
so the kingdom of God is present now just as Jesus is
present. His presence is the essence of the kingdom. But
Jesus has yet to come in his full glory and power to
consummate his kingdom and bring justice and peace to
every corner of the universe. In the coming of Jesus in the
incarnation, his kingdom was fulfilled, but it is yet to be
consummated. This distinction is critical. The kingdom
of God is present, but so is the kingdom of darkness.
Jesus came and announced that God's kingdom is at
hand, but the victory over the forces of evil is not yet
complete.

This image of the Christian life, then, reminds us that
believers live in a dynamic tension. Christians live in two

worlds, two realities at the same time. We are citizens of both earth and heaven, and until the final consummation of the kingdom, when earth and heaven are one, we live constantly in the midst of spiritual warfare. This warfare is both internal (the battle for our minds) and external (the battle for justice and peace in the social structures of our world). The latter is a battle for Christian priorities and values as distinctives in society—our cultural, social, and political identity. The former is the believer's battle for a renewed mind. Naturally, the two spheres are linked. God's kingdom rule in our society is highly dependent on his kingdom rule in our minds. But the renewal of our minds is not possible if we ignore social, intellectual, and economic issues. The two spheres are mutually dependent.

Loss of appreciation for the kingdom will consistently lead to a warped spirituality. In some cases, it has led to a wholly inward and individual spirituality that ignores social and economic injustices as well as the predicament of a neighbor who has not heard the gospel. The loss of a kingdom awareness has led others to an uncritical acceptance of social and cultural perspectives, so that Christianity has been identified with political movements or cultural ideals. Ultimately, the gospel suffers.

Others, in neglecting the centrality of the kingdom, have advocated an otherworldly spirituality that ignores the world and teaches that the Christian has no ultimate identity with or responsibility for the created order.

But a recovery of the centrality of this motif can give the Christian community a vitally needed perspective on the world. If we are to have an authentic spirituality in the world, we need to recover a vision of the Christian life that encompasses all of creation—that of the kingdom of God.

IMPLICATIONS OF THE KINGDOM FOR A CHRISTIAN SPIRITUALITY

We can identify three critical implications of the kingdom image for Christians. Each is a factor in our understanding of our activity in the world.

A New Perspective on Vocation

First, a recovery of centrality of the kingdom will free the Christian community to hear the call of God upon its members to a wide variety of vocations. God is calling men and women to infiltrate the camp of the enemy. Men and women are called to business, education, politics, the arts, and sciences as well as to professional Christian ministry. The notion that professional ministry is a higher calling or superior vocation should be forever banished from our thinking. All vocations are kingdom vocations. All Christians are kingdom agents within their vocations as Christ uses all as his instruments of light, his ambassadors of reconciliation.

Consequently, it is critical that we assist all Christians in discerning their vocations and then, through the ministry of the church, equip them to fulfill their callings (Eph. 4:12ff.). The world has yet to witness the impact of a community of worshiping believers who gather together to encourage and equip one another for service within those God-given vocations. The Christian community can be salt and light within society only insofar as men and women are freed to respond to the full range of vocations for which God has enlisted his people.

As we seek to identify the essential components of a Christian spirituality, we do so with the full acknowledgment that different vocations require a different spirituality. The components are essential. The forms in which these components are found will vary from individual to individual, and a fundamental factor in shaping a spirituality will be the matter of vocation.

A New Perspective on Time

Second, a recovery of the centrality of the kingdom will give the Christian community a renewed perspective on time. Generally speaking, there are two classic heresies with respect to an understanding of time. Some view all meaningful time as future. They live for the future. The present is merely a stepping-stone for the future, and all their energies are devoted to accomplishing something yet ahead of them in time. Their vision arises out of a conviction that great things can be accomplished for God, and they view time as wasted when it is not used in practical ways that meet goals and objectives. The heresy here is that this perspective on time denies that the kingdom has come. Regardless of how wonderful plans and goals may be, the kingdom is present. Jesus has come; the Incarnation led to the death and resurrection of the Christ! We can relax; Christ is Lord! Consequently, our work or activity in this world is not merely a means to an end. It glorifies God in itself. It can be a joyful foretaste of the consummated kingdom. We distort time when we are driven to work purely to have something in the future.

But then there are those for whom the future can wait. They love life and probably feel that the future will be what it will be. They will live tomorrow, tomorrow. They appreciate the seasons of life, the daily routine of work and friends and food. They feel a peace with God and with creation. They are convinced that there is time enough for everything. But this, too, is a heresy, a partial truth. The kingdom is not yet consummated. The sin lurking within our minds and the horrendous injustices that characterize our societies are surely daily and sufficient reminders that we must be about the Master's business.

The solution to these two heresies is found in a renewed appreciation of the Incarnation and the kingdom. In the Incarnation, we have the union of time and eternity in the person of Christ Jesus. In the Incarnation, we have the union of the mystical and the earthly. In Christ, we have the fulfillment of the kingdom. But though the kingdom will be consummated in Christ, we stand now in a tension between fulfillment and consummation. We must therefore have both a present and a future orientation. We can live in peace and rest in the confidence that the kingdom has come; we also need to live with a holy dissatisfaction with the circumstances around us and strive in the grace of God to be agents of kingdom redemption.

Time is so frequently viewed as a nonrenewable resource. But think about this for a moment. Regardless of how you respond to the next hour in your life, you will have just as many hours left in your day. Time is a gift from God, an opportunity to be responded to. It is more helpful to think of time as something that is filled rather than as something that is used. Then instead of bemoaning the passing of time, you can delight in each new moment, each new day, each new season. You can accept time and the passing of years graciously.

In this perspective, then, a spirituality is merely a structure or a routine for responding joyfully and effectively to the gift of time. We need to be preserved from the tendency to passionately rush through time and thereby miss the voice of God and the signs of the kingdom. But we need equally to be preserved from the life that fails to fulfill its potential. We are called to abide in Christ as well as serve Christ. Joy and effectiveness within our vocations come from a gentle and steady rhythm of abiding in the Lord, on the one hand, and serving the Lord, on the other.

A Unifying Principle for the Christian Life

Third, a recovery of the centrality of the kingdom to a Christian spirituality will help the Christian community recover a unity in the Christian life. It is tragic when so many Christians recognize there are different elements to their lives but fail to discover an abiding unity among them. They see themselves within a wide variety of roles, perhaps as father, doctor, church deacon, and husband. But what is the focus, the unity principle, that brings all these roles together? Others may recognize clearly that their lives have both private and public dimensions, times of solitude and times of community, times of personal struggle and times when they feel the weight of nuclear threat or social oppression. But again, what is the unity among these diverse concerns in an individual life?

The image of the kingdom can effectively serve as that unifying principle when it complements the mystical-relational images presented in the previous chapter. Through the image of the kingdom, we recognize that spirituality can no longer be viewed as merely touching upon the religious dimensions of life. Suddenly, the spiritual is not just what we do in the prayer closet or with fellow believers during public worship. True spirituality is kingdom living, which of necessity means that we can see God in the whole of our lives, in private and in public, at work and in the home, in the church and in the street, and even at play—whether with children, in sports activities, or in some form of healthy entertainment. The kingdom becomes the unifying principle that brings together every dimension of our lives.

Consequently, we are freed from the oppressive burden that religious activities are somehow more important than the mundane ordinary life of domestic activities and work. If all comes under the kingdom, religious activities are surely important. But not all life is religion! We are members of families. We have occupations and responsibilities in our places of work. We have leisure time to enjoy friends, hobbies, and the arts. If we deny or undermine the other dimensions of our lives, we subtly ignore the centrality of the kingdom in God's redemptive plan.

This study, in identifying the essential components of a Christian spirituality, assumes that we are attempting to see the whole of life under a unifying principle. All of life becomes spiritual. The whole of life, each dimension, is lived in terms of the kingdom and therefore is an aspect of spirituality. True spirituality is the whole of life lived in relationship with the divine Trinity—a mystical relationship. It is also the whole of life lived in the world under the kingdom rule of God.

EVALUATING MODELS OF THE SPIRITUAL LIFE

It should be evident by now that a model of the Christian life needs to have theological integrity. As we reflect on our own Christian lives and think about Christian spirituality based on the various books we read or sermons we hear or hymns we sing, we need to have a basis for any assessment we might make. We need some basis for evaluating whether a spirituality is theologically sound or not. I have suggested that an authentic Christian spirituality must include a mystical dimension, with an emphasis on a personal relationship with the holy Trinity. It must also emphasize a full-orbed understanding of the world and the Christian's relationship to that world. The unifying principle between these two dimensions is the Incarnation.

Robert Webber, in his work *Common Roots: A Call to Evangelical Maturity*, has made the helpful suggestion that we need to recover and appreciate the implications of the Incarnation for a Christian spirituality.[1] In Christ, the mystical and the earthly come together, the divine and the human. We are in the domain of heresy when either the human or the divine is emphasized at the neglect of the other. Similarly, the Incarnation itself can be the standard for evaluating a spirituality and recovering a true spirituality that is both mystical and earthly.

Webber suggests that there are three essential features of an incarnational spirituality. I will add a fourth. First, a spiritual life that is lived in terms of the Incarnation affirms that Christ is the spirituality. To be a Christian is to be found in Christ, before God. Furthermore, the spirituality must be Christocentric. The life, death, and resurrection of Christ define what it means to be a Christian and make the Christian life possible. Webber rightly stresses the Reformational principle that the Christian is "simul justus et peccator." The Christian is a saint because in Christ the believer is acceptable before God. But the Christian is also a sinner because the outworking of God's grace is as yet incomplete. The Christian life is, consequently, lived in continual gratitude and humility. Further, growth in grace is always in terms of the Christ event. The Christian life is lived historically in terms of the person and work of Jesus—his life, death, and resurrection in the past, and the personal return and consummation of his kingdom in the future.

The astonishing truth of the Incarnation is that in and through Christ, we can enter into a personal, mystical relationship with the living God. Prayer and worship have meaning because of Christ. He is the ascended Lord, who has served as our perfect mediator, and who now ever intercedes for us. Jesus broke the impasse between heaven and earth, making a relationship with God possible.

Second, an incarnational spirituality affirms that the

Christian life is a response to God in the church. The church is the body of Christ—the visible, living presence of the incarnate Lord in the world. Christ communicates his word and grace through the ministry of the church, specifically the corporate life and ministry of believers, the preaching and teaching of the Word, the sacraments, prayer, and worship. True spirituality is not merely oriented to the individual. It is life in community.

Third, the Incarnation makes it very plain that a true spirituality is a response to God in the world. This implies that the world is created by God and is intended to be the sphere of God's rule. Through redemptive work in Christ, God intends to bring all things under his kingdom rule. True spirituality, then, is not escapist. We cannot view the Christian life as something lived outside this world or in anticipation of an otherworldly kingdom. Our salvation is very earthly. A true spirituality is driven by a concern to find visible expression of God's goodness and justice in the world. A spirituality that encourages an abandonment of the world cannot be called Christian. Further, we recognize that though this is our Father's world, the prince of darkness is actively at work in this world to undermine God's kingdom. Consequently, an incarnational spirituality affirms the reality of spiritual warfare.

Finally, an incarnational spirituality recognizes that there is a need for structure, order, and routine in the Christian life. We are not angels. We are flesh-and-blood creatures, and our understanding of spirituality need make no apology for our physical state. That is how we were created. But in affirming our bodies, we need to recognize that our very humanity must define our spirituality. When we pray, we do not pray as angels. We are embodied souls. A spirituality that fails to recognize and appreciate our full humanity inadvertently denies that Christ Jesus came in the flesh. An affirmation of Christ's humanity, and therefore our own, frees us to appreciate the significance of space and time for the Christian life.

For example, prayer, meditation, reflection, and study are best nurtured in an atmosphere of quiet. Yet urban life is noisy, which encourages superficiality. Reflection on the deeper meaning and significance of our lives requires retreat. Prayer prospers in a quiet chapel; careful study is easier in an orderly, silent library. True corporate worship includes the affirmation that the worshipers are seeing, hearing, and smelling creatures. We do not worship merely as souls. What we see, hear, smell, and even taste affects our response to God in worship.

When my children were much younger, we had the privilege of visiting the magnificent Cologne Cathedral, which is perhaps the highest cathedral in Europe. It was windy and blustery in Cologne on that spring day, and we were feeling the chill as we came in the main entrance. Immediately, we sensed the hush in the high vault. We walked in only about twenty feet and stopped, the four of us, and looked up. After a minute or so, one of my sons spoke.

"Dad, I'm afraid," he said. And I understood. There was an incredible silence within that space—not a magical silence, nothing spooky, just a quiet magnificence, captured by the architect in the space he had created. Architecture affects our understanding and sense of God because we are embodied souls; our spiritual response to God is shaped by physical realities. This applies equally to the corporate, public worship as much as to our private prayers.

But more, it applies to each of the disciplines of the spiritual life. The acts by which we appropriate the grace of God are essentially actions of our bodies, our whole beings, in patterns and in response to God's grace. We are embodied souls, and so we need structure, routine, and order to properly nurture our relationship with the living God and our kingdom activity in the world.

Part 2 of this reflective study will be an examination of five classic disciplines of the spiritual life. In each case I will suggest that through discipline we can know God and his grace. Each discipline will be explained, and suggestions will be given for its implementation into the fabric of our lives.

PART TWO

The Five Essential Components of a Christian Spirituality

CHAPTER 6

The Renewal of the Mind

There are five essential components of a Christian spirituality. The first is the renewal of the mind.

THE NEED FOR MENTAL RENEWAL

To be Christian we must think Christianly. To walk in the Spirit requires a spiritual mind. Our transformation into the image of God depends on renewed minds. The Bible calls us to love God with our whole minds. Consequently, *the* critical component of a Christian spirituality is care for our thinking. It is not possible to think of being Christian without realizing that fundamental to walking with Christ is the renewing of the mind.

The Bible clearly assumes the need for and calls for the renewal of the mind. We find this throughout Scripture, but the call is most notable in the writings of the apostle Paul. It is in his letters we find the exhortation to be transformed by the renewing of our minds (Rom. 12:1–2).

The Apostle also urges us not to be taken captive through deceptive philosophy, which he identifies as the basic principles of this world (Col. 2:8). We cannot grow in Christ if we allow the world to shape the way we think, if our values, norms, and worldview are determined by our culture.

The Bible calls us to turn. Repentance includes turning in the way we think—a change of mind. Those who are not in Christ are described by Paul as darkened in the way they think; those who are in Christ are urged to set their minds on things above (Col. 3:2), being renewed in knowledge, after the image of the Creator (Col. 3:10). This largely involves allowing the Word of Christ to dwell richly within the mind (Col. 3:16). This is conversion—the turning from an unspiritual mind (Col. 2:18) with the goal that every thought be taken captive and made obedient to Christ (2 Cor. 10:5).

What we think is what we are. Unless we are renewed in the attitudes of the mind, in the way we think, we cannot hope to become what God would like us to be. The mind is the steering wheel of the person. It is only as our minds are renewed and controlled by the Spirit that we can hope to become mature in our faith. But it is a matter of discipline.

Some may think that the call for a renewed mind applies only to intellectuals or academics—that it is not as applicable to those who do not feel they are very intelligent. But Paul makes no such distinction between the intelligent and the not-so-intelligent. Rather, Scripture assumes that all people are intelligent. That is what it means to be a person—a thinking, rational being.

All people can think and know. All Christians can come to love God with their whole minds. Each person, in Christ, can come to have a mind renewed according to the image of Christ. The renewal of the mind is a concern much broader than the intellectual or academic life in society. Academic study may be helpful, but renewal of the mind is essential for all thinking people—that is, all people. As the Apostle puts it in his letter to the Romans, it is only as our minds are transformed that we are able to discern the will of God and know what is good, acceptable, and perfect (Rom. 12:1–2).

There are two aspects of this mental renewal. The first is the renewal of the *way* in which we think. The second relates to *what* we are thinking about, the focus of our thoughts. The full and extended renewal of the mind involves both dimensions.

The Way We Think

Few people recognize how they think. Thinking is not usually something that we think about! We just do it. And that is the problem. We will not be renewed in the way we think unless we give it serious attention. A Christian mind has come to think in terms of and according to the truth. It is a mind that understands life as God sees life. We seek the mind of God, which means that we want to think God's thoughts and see the world, ourselves, our society, our past, and our future as he sees these realities.

Somehow, we need to recognize that before we came to Christ, our thinking was warped. We saw and thought and understood things, but we did not see reality in the right perspective. Our thinking lacked the most important dimension—God. Growing in grace, therefore, means growing up and turning around in the way that we think. It means coming to a deeper and fuller understanding of the truth, the way God sees things. We can live in freedom only when we see and understand as God sees. In other words, we need to adopt a Christian worldview.

What We Think About

We need to be renewed in the way we think but also in the focus of our thoughts—what we think about. We are called by the apostle Paul to "think about these things," the true, the honorable, the right, the pure, the lovely, the admirable, the excellent—all that is worthy of praise (Phil. 4:8–9). If we are what we think, we need to be careful what we think about.

The mind is an amazing thing. It is our most private space. When it comes to the focus of our thoughts, we are all individuals, standing alone and choosing what we will think about. A doctor can look inside my body and tell me what my heart is doing and what my kidneys are doing. But my mind is my private space.

The mind is also amazing in that it never stops working. The mind is active even when we sleep. The mind is affecting the direction of our lives even when we are not thinking about such profound questions. But what do we think about? Or to put it another way, what do we think about when we have nothing to think about? What passes through our thoughts when we are riding the bus to a place of work or going to a store to do some shopping?

What is happening in our minds when we are just waiting? It is at these times as much as any other that we need to recognize the importance of discipline. We cannot know the peace of God and be renewed in our thinking unless we allow the Spirit to control our minds. And this includes consciously directing our thoughts to what is "worthy of praise."

Even as we go to sleep at night, the mind will focus on thoughts that dominate our thinking before we actually fall asleep. We are, therefore, urged to give special attention to these moments in the day and settle our thoughts, possibly through the Word, on what is good, honorable, and just.

Our goal is the biblical ideal of a renewed mind. The concept that captures this for us in Scripture is that of the "mind of Christ." We are called to have attitudes that are in accordance with Christ's mind. Kosuke Koyama suggests that by implication we are called to have crucified minds. In contrast, much of Western Christianity, as it has encountered the East, has been governed by a crusading mind, which summarizes in many respects the ideals of Western culture with its aggressiveness and sense of manifest destiny. But as Koyama notes, this attitude of mind is utterly opposed to the gospel.[1]

The attitudes of gratitude, humility, service, and hope mark the Christian mind as summarized in the call to love as God has loved us. Armando Vallardares was imprisoned for twenty-three years in the brutal, inhuman Cuban prison system. He languished there year after year, suffering incredible abuse because of his convictions. He refused to compromise with his accusers and consequently faced the fury of a regime intolerant of dissenters. How did he survive with sound mind and spirit for twenty-three years? His biography, *Against All Hope,* provides many clues.[2] It lay in his faith in God, in his personal commitment to live by his conscience, in his persistent hope, and in his willingness to forgive his tormentors. The answer to his remarkable perseverance lies in his mind—a mind guarded and supported by divine grace.

A Christian mind is a mind pervaded by peace. It is a peace that transcends understanding (Phil. 4:7). But this characteristic feature of the Christian mind comes only to those who choose to live in joy, not in anxiety, casting their cares on God. The peace of God is a gift to those who discipline their minds to think those things worthy of praise.

THE MIND, OUR CULTURE, AND TELEVISION

What shapes the human mind? The human mind, by its very nature, is conditioned by outside stimuli; it is not self-contained. The mind can think only in terms of what we feed into it. For instance, a computer is a wonderful thing. But it is useless unless it has a powerful and helpful program that can be booted into the system. Similarly, the mind functions constantly on the basis of what we allow it to receive. Part of personal discipline is determining what will and what will not enter the mind.

We need to decide: Will our minds be filled with the values and perspectives of our society and culture (that is, the world), or will our minds be richly indwelt by the Word of God? It is not a moot question for the simple reason that our minds are being shaped whether we are conscious of it or not.

Christians in the twentieth century need to deal with the issue of television viewing. The television is the most significant factor shaping the mind of many contemporary societies. It is one of the most powerful forces in the battle for the mind, and the mind of the Christian is often a battleground between the television and its values and the preacher's sermon on Sunday morning.

Jeanne Cover, writing in *Religious Education*, effectively shows how TV advertising and most TV programs essentially desensitize our vision and imagination and form priorities. The problem, Cover argues, is that the values portrayed through the television medium are nonbiblical—commitment in marriage is trivialized, religion is downplayed, illicit relationships are accepted, violence is condoned, and a variety of commercial products are portrayed as essential for personal dignity, happiness, meaning, and success. While it is true that TV may well reflect the breakdown of family life and commitment in relationships, the unnerving truth is that TV advertising and programming legitimize this deterioration. Cover concludes,

> We have now come to accept the priorities and attitudes of the powerful that permeate our televised lives—success, affluence, private property, efficiency and competition, consumerism, and the "advantages" of technology. The marketplace precepts have come to be given a universal validity.[3]

In other words, the TV does not merely entertain. It creates attitudes and priorities, and it portrays a view of life dominated by consumerism.

We need to realize that television is an entertainment medium. Many attempt to use it for other purposes. Jacques Cousteau uses the TV to bring people to an awareness of the oceans of the world; TV evangelists seek to lead people to a knowledge of Christ. But it is an entertainment medium. As Neil Postman so cogently notes, using TV as an educational medium is as absurd as using a 747 airplane to deliver mail between New York City and Newark (twin cities). It is the wrong medium for the purpose.[4]

The TV is imagistic. Our analytical, linear thought processes are bypassed. We do not think when we watch TV. We are entertained. We are passive recipients of whatever is shown to us. The influence of TV, then, is not only subtle and direct; it is also pervasive and, to a remarkable degree, subconscious. It permeates the mind and radically affects the way in which a person perceives the world and discriminates between good and evil.

This has particular relevance as we wrestle with the reality of sexual drive and marital fidelity. Television blatantly and subtly caters to prurient sexual interests and curiosity. It trivializes and makes our God-given sexuality mundane by affirming immediate gratification.

Television advertising panders to our greed, our desire to impress, the longing for comfort and amenities. Rarely does TV advertising assume we are intelligent, thinking persons. Rather, its purpose is to bypass our rational faculties and get us to buy or consume some-thing, regardless of whether we really need to.

What is alarming is that this happens when our guard is down, when we are being "entertained." For many, it comes after a difficult day of work. TV viewing is an evening activity for relaxation and leisure. It may be the single most significant influence on the way people, even Christians, think. Their devotional life, their participation in public worship (including the sermon), and other valuable input, such as Bible study, cannot offset the far more pervasive influence of TV. In other words, TV is the dominant stimulus and shaper of their lives, so much so that they cannot be richly indwelt by the Word.

TV is really one of several influences, but it is singled out because of its pervasive effects on the mind of urban societies. We are no longer shocked by violence we repeatedly see; we are no longer shamed by sexual explicitness; we are humored through repeated viewing of what is explicitly contrary to our declared values. We must seriously consider what does shape the way we think as we respond to the call to renew the mind.

THE SHAPING OF THE MIND: THE IMPACT OF SCRIPTURE

Physically, we develop appetites for certain foods. Some time ago my wife, Joella, decided it was not good to have so much salt in our family's diet. So she resolved to gradually cut our salt intake over a short period of time to a bare minimum. At first I thought that food would be tasteless without salt, that like all other spices, salt was essential for flavor. But I learned otherwise; I am enjoying my food as much as ever but without the harmful effects of too much salt. Now I am amazed at how people pour salt on their food; when I eat food that has too much salt, I find it difficult to consume. Similarly, I no longer take sugar in my tea or coffee. I resolved to go off this unnecessary sweet, and now my taste buds no longer crave sugar.

The same applies to the intellect. When we feed our minds with garbage, we develop an appetite for it. It is not good to saturate our minds with television imagery with its violence, sexual explicitness, and bland humor. The danger is that we develop an unhealthy taste for it. An appetite for truth, for the good, the noble, and the honorable, takes time to develop. But we cannot hope to have renewed minds unless we resolve to desire what is good and true, unless we allow the Spirit to transform our intellectual appetites.

The most important way by which the mind is renewed is through the Scriptures. Paul calls us to a mind renewed after the image of its Creator, largely by letting the Word of Christ dwell richly in our minds (Col. 3:10, 16).

There is more to the full renewal of the mind than merely the indwelling of Scripture. The arts, travel, study within the humanities and the sciences, good conversation, and much more contribute to a renewed mind. Scripture is focused on here because of space limitations and the recognition of its primary role in the renewal of the mind.

God has provided us, through the Scriptures, with his

perspective on life. We are free in the way we think only when we think according to the truth. The renewal of the mind is intimately linked with the knowledge of God through his Word. But this must be a pervasive and experiential knowledge. It is not merely a matter of intellectual understanding, though this is a critical component. We are called to have minds that are richly indwelt by the Word. This is what we seek—minds that are governed by the thoughts of God.

All disciplines of the spiritual life are designed to foster the renewal of the mind, but some of them are more directly and immediately linked with this element of a Christian spirituality. I will identify two.

Scripture

The first is the discipline of *Bible reading, study, and memorization*. We need to be men and women of the Word, and there is no shortcut to the knowledge and understanding of Scripture. If we believe that the Bible is the Word of God, we can come to the Scriptures with that assumption and receive it as divine revelation— nothing less. The ideal would be to establish a pattern of daily Bible reading and memorization—reading with care, conscious that the original meaning of the text is largely determined by the context.

Another particularly valuable practice is to take a two- to three-hour period for extended reading. Christians often misuse the Bible by building up their knowledge of Scripture around verses and phrases rather than broader portions. Rarely do we read the Epistles in one sitting, as they were written. We draw new insight when we read a gospel in one sitting, and we appreciate the dramatic growth of the early church as we read the book of Acts in one sitting. Many Christians commend the practice of reading through the Bible regularly—some have suggested reading the Scripture from Genesis through Revelation at least once every five years.

Christians of all ages have also commended the practice of Scripture memorization. Start with a little, perhaps, but begin. A verse a day is a minimum—but build on this. There is probably no spiritual discipline that so effectively leads to the indwelling of the mind with the Word of Christ as the practice of consistent memorization.

Study

The second discipline directed specifically to the renewal of the mind is *study* that reflects on the application of biblical truth to life. We passionately seek the truth, with the confidence that we cannot know freedom unless we know the truth. Our longing is for our minds to know, understand, and live according to the truth. Study, in this respect, is a spiritual discipline.

There are two simple but complementary steps in study. The first is acquisition of the facts. The second is reflection on the facts and their interrelationship or correlation. Here we ask, "What do the facts mean?"; "What significance do they have?" We interpret the facts in terms of our own experience and in light of our previous study. Both steps are essential for the study to have spiritual benefit.

Our study can and needs to lead us into the truth in

each of the dimensions of our lives. First, as Christians we should constantly explore the full range of Christian doctrine, deepening our appreciation of the faith. Next, we need to study the faith with specific reference to vocation. For instance, the doctor is particularly concerned with the relationship between faith and medical practice; the teacher seeks a biblical understanding of the student as a learner and the task of communicating truth. Third, all Christians need to be stretching their minds to appreciate the implications of divine revelation for life (ethics). For example, to a husband and a father, what does the Word say and mean for someone who has these relationships? As a member of society and a person who bears responsibility in society, what does the Word say about the Christian in the world?

Fortunately, in the task of study we do not stand alone. We stand within a community of faith, and superb literature on every facet of doctrine and life is available. In time we come to identify authors who are particularly helpful in the task of searching for the truth. The discipline of study includes the study of Scripture as well as the careful reading and study of books that can assist us in our quest.

Constantly, we keep our goal before us. We are seeking to be conformed to the image of Christ and maintain our union with him. For this we aspire after the renewal of our minds and respond to this need with study that fosters this goal.

CHAPTER 7

Personal Encounter with God

THE CALL TO PRAYER AND SOLITUDE

*T*he second component of an authentic Christian spirituality is a pattern of formal prayer and worship. This is probably the component most often associated with religious life. Some may even conclude that being Christian means being like everyone else except that a Christian adds religious activities to the daily schedule—notably prayer and worship. This is not an accurate perception, of course. True spirituality is much more—but it just as surely includes these elements. If we are going to serve God in the demanding and difficult setting to which he has called us, we can be satisfied with nothing less than a consistent and authentic encounter with God—personally, in our private prayers, and publicly, as members of the church through the act of worship.

In the gospel of Mark, chapter 1, we read of an interesting encounter between Jesus and his disciple, Peter. Very early in the morning, while it was still dark (v. 35), Jesus left the home he was staying in and went off to spend some time in prayer and solitude. Peter and his companions went looking for him. Jesus was in demand, we read. It seems the whole town was eager to find him. He was needed, desperately needed. Peter could hardly suppress his frustration that Jesus was not present when he was needed. "Everyone is looking for you," Peter announced, amazed that Jesus was so difficult to find.

In the next verses we discover two abiding features of Jesus' ministry that are the direct result of his commitment to a life of prayer in solitude. First, Jesus did not respond to the demands and the pleas of the townspeople of Capernaum. Rather, he calmly announced that he had to go to other villages to preach, for that was his calling. Second, we note in the verses that follow, Jesus was filled with compassion and reached out to touch a desperately needy leprous man.

The evidence is clear. Jesus' strength of ministry and depth of compassion are both directly related to the consistency and vitality of his personal prayer life. Jesus led a life that routinely included encounter with his heavenly Father. Formal prayer and worship were well-established habits in the life of our Lord.

Nothing guarantees a personal encounter with God. An intimate and profound sense of the presence of God is sheer gift. But the testimony of our spiritual forefathers and mothers and the common experience of believers of all ages, cultures, and backgrounds confirm that when men and women eagerly dispose themselves to such an encounter, in the context of prayer and worship to hear his Word and receive his grace, God is more than willing to encounter his people.

An authentic Christian life is actually inconceivable apart from an established pattern of formal prayer and worship. Prayer and worship are not only important and obvious features of Jesus' life and ministry. Every significant church leader and spiritual director throughout the history of the church confirms again and again through writings and example that this pattern is crucial.

The component of formal prayer and worship includes the personal/private as well as the corporate/public. Healthy spirituality depends on both dimensions. For the purposes of this discussion, however, I will focus on the personal and private.

PRIVATE, FORMAL PRAYER AND SOLITUDE

This component of the Christian life is based on a simple principle: There is no growth in the spiritual life without time spent alone with God. Solitude is essential to deepening the interior life. It is a means of coming to an intimate knowledge of God. By faith, we affirm the possibility of meeting God through private prayer; we also recognize that through this encounter, we become new people, who are more fully able to be God's kingdom agents in the world.

A constant danger, though, is that we would become legalistic about the form a personal, formal prayer time should take. I remember reading a booklet early in my Christian life that suggested all committed Christians devote the first hour of the day to God. The message I got was that commitment is reflected in one's willingness to spend early morning time in prayer—the earlier, the better. Well, if I was not a committed Christian, I wanted to be, and so I began a regimen of early morning rising, striving to stay awake, meditating on a passage of Scripture, and interceding for my needs and those of others. But it was agony. More often than not I lived in guilt because of a lack of a meaningful prayer experience. I grew to hate prayer; it was a burden.

Later I came to realize that a better guiding rule is that we should give God the best time of our day—and by best, I mean that hour when we are most alert. Different people have different physical metabolisms. Some individuals are more awake in the morning, others in the late evening. Each person needs to decide which time of the day is most profitable. For some, the time may need to vary because of changes in personal schedule.

Though we cannot be legalistic about the specific form that a personal, private time of prayer should have, the weight of our spiritual heritage would support the idea that setting aside between a half hour and an hour is both wise and reasonable. Some could perhaps live with less time in prayer; others will need more. Most of us need that much time to still our minds, renew our sense of perspective, meaningfully meditate on and respond to a portion of Scripture, reflect on who we are and what God is doing in our lives, and hear a word from God.

We need to actively work against the idea that we are too busy for extended prayer time. Few elements of our spiritual lives will prove our mettle as much as our willingness to spend time with God. Does it not seem ironic that we sometimes act as if God has given us so much to do that we can no longer spend extended time with him? Isn't the lack of a significant, consistent pattern of personal, formal prayer a sign that much of our work, our business, is our own doing and not the will of God? It is inconceivable to think God would give us so much to do that we can no longer spend extended time with him.

John Carmody quotes an Eastern theologian who notes, "When the devil wants to detach someone from the one thing necessary, he occupies him with a lot of work which does not leave him a free moment for meditation or for deepening his interior life."[1] This is a strong reminder that we need to place a fence around some period in our daily schedule to meet alone with God. This applies particularly to urban dwellers. The busyness and superficiality of city life make it particularly urgent that we establish a pattern for personal, private prayer.

We need to find a place of quiet for an effective and consistent encounter with God. Our internal space is notably affected by external space. Noise and confusion around us are not conducive to inner peace and reflection. We are embodied souls. For an extended time of quiet, we need space. Crucial to this component of an authentic Christian spirituality is that we find a private space where we can regularly encounter our God.

A STRUCTURE OR PATTERN FOR OUR PRAYER

There are many ways in which an hour of prayer could be structured. (See suggested format for an hour of daily formal prayer in Appendix 1.) But the accumulated wisdom of our spiritual heritage teaches that some basic elements can make prayer more fruitful. First, it is particularly helpful to begin the hour through a conscious centering of our thoughts. Our busy minds need to be stilled; the turmoil of our hearts needs to be quieted so that we can pray. A favorite psalm or a well-known hymn is helpful for centering; for some, a brief prayer of submission to the spirit of God brings their thoughts in focus and opens the mind to hear God's Word.

Second, the hour could include a time of meditation on a text of Scripture. Ideally, the text should be one in which most of the basic questions on its interpretation have already been answered. It is not too beneficial, in terms of prayer, if we meditate on a text we do not understand. Further, it is probably obvious that God's word to us is consistent with the word of Scripture. Therefore, we would be wise to meditate on portions of Scripture we have studied and come to a basic understanding about. We don't want to meditate on a promise in Scripture, hear it as God's word to us, and then find out later that the promise was taken out of context and applies only to the original audience.

Next, the time in prayer needs to include the element of communion, preferably found in a time of extended silence in the presence of the Lord. The time of prayer is literally a time with God. We are not in prayer just to receive our marching orders; neither is it merely a time for repentance. These elements will be a part of prayer, but a time alone with God, an hour of solitude in our prayer closet (Matt. 6:6), is more than anything else a time of fellowship with God himself. Our prayer experience is governed by the Word of God; the God we meet reveals himself through the Scriptures. But this is not a time of communion with the Scriptures. It is, very simply, a time of encounter with God. As such, we need to consciously set aside the Bible and with minds that are filled with that Word enjoy the presence of God and delight in his company.

The goal of our time with God is to come to know him. But though this knowledge is grounded in the Word, and it is an understanding based on truth, the knowledge we seek is experiential. Our longing is to be a people who know God—and we come to know God, individually, through this personal encounter in the solitude of our prayers.

In knowing God and hearing his Word, we choose then, out of silence, to respond. There are four classic responses: adoration, thanksgiving, confession, and care-casting. Prayer can be a response appropriate to the text we have been meditating on and the word we have heard in our silence. In knowing God, we come to know ourselves, and these classic responses to God's Word are also expressions of who we are.

KNOWING OURSELVES AS GOD KNOWS US

Lack of self-knowledge is one of the profound effects of the Fall. Sin leads us to self-deception. In contrast, the hope of the new heavens and the new earth is that we will know fully even as we are fully known (1 Cor. 13:12). Through the personal encounter with God in formal prayer, one of the most significant benefits of knowing God is that we come to know ourselves as well. This self-knowledge is a gift from God—but we learn from the spiritual leaders of the church that there are exercises of prayer that can free us to receive this gift.

First, we can respond to God with *adoration*. If he revealed something about himself that deeply impresses us, whether it is his wisdom, goodness, beauty, or power, we need to allow our hearts to burst forth in response, allowing the fullness of our hearts to be expressed in adoration. We know ourselves, in part, through a recognition of what creates awe and wonder within us.

Second, self-knowledge is enhanced through the spiritual exercise of *thanksgiving*. When we start reflecting on God's goodness to us, we are soon freed from a heavy spirit. Praise is most meaningful when it arises in response to God's goodness to us—as we feel and experience his mercy. Ultimately, we thank him for his greatest gift, the person of Jesus Christ.

Third, self-knowledge includes *confession of sin*, an awareness of where we have failed in the eyes of God. Knowing God cannot help lighting up our own character and behavior. An awareness of his presence consistently leads us to confess we have fallen short of his ideal for us. But it is most helpful to think of our confession as a reflection of God's assessment of us. It is not so much a self-examination as it is an opening up to God for him to reveal his purposes for us. Each of us should ask, "God, how do you see me? Where do you feel I need to grow and turn from sin?" In the end, this form of confession bears the greatest fruit and has the most potential to assist us toward spiritual maturity.

Finally, a time of prayer can include the spiritual exercise of *care-casting*.[2] One of our vulnerable areas in spiritual warfare is fear or worry. There is a real sense in which our greatest fear is also our weakest point for attack by the evil one. Conversely, God exhorts us in his Word to cast all our cares upon him. We are invited to place all our anxieties upon his shoulders. There is no reason for us to worry, for he is committed to caring for us. In giving him our cares, we can know his peace, which transcends understanding (Phil. 4:6–7; 1 Peter 5:7).

Many years ago, when traveling in Canada from Calgary, Alberta, to Kamloops, British Columbia, we had been on the road for less than a half hour when Micah, our younger boy, asked where we would be spending the night. I told him it would be in Kamloops, after six or seven hours of driving. But that did not satisfy him, and he asked again. So I told him, "At a motel in Kamloops, Micah."

"But, Dad, *which* motel?" he wanted to know.

"I do not know, son. *Some* motel, *any* motel," I replied.

"But how do you know a motel will be there?"

Well, my dear son had grown up in the Philippines and did not realize, I thought, that every little town in Canada has a motel; and Kamloops, a good size city, would have plenty of motels. But he was still not reassured. I was feeling a little frustrated with him, but I turned and said, "Micah, let me worry about this. You sit in the back and enjoy the trip. Your dad will worry about where we spend the night."

And that was all he needed. He relaxed and immediately stopped bothering me. Then I saw what had happened. It was an entirely reasonable concern, the matter of where we would spend the night. But it was too big a matter for a six-year-old to be worried about. Similarly, our Father in heaven loves to receive us and hear of our deepest fears and concerns. It is not that concerns and fears are not valid. They are real areas of concern; we are worried about our well-being and the welfare of those we love. My son was concerned about where we would sleep. It was an authentic matter to be worried about; it was not an infantile concern. But as a child, he did not need to fret. His mind was unable to handle it. Similarly, as creatures of our heavenly Father, we worry about concerns that are too big for us, and he bids us cast all of our cares upon him. They are important matters, but his word to us is that he will carry them.

Each of these four classic responses to the Lord in prayer may also serve suitably as a means of centering our thoughts as we begin our hour. If our minds are filled with awe in response to the beauty of God's creation, it is appropriate to begin our prayers with adoration. We can begin with thanksgiving in response to the goodness of God. If there is sin or an anxiety disturbing the spirit, it is essential that we resolve these concerns even as we enter our prayers, and in so doing, we will be centering our thoughts.

Not all of these elements for knowing God and ourselves would be included each day in prayer. Rather, it is helpful to see these spiritual exercises as resources upon which we can draw as we pray. As we do, we will find that the prayer time is consistently more fruitful.

DISCERNMENT, INTERCESSION, AND RENEWED COMMITMENT

Prayer thus far has strengthened our communion with God. We know God and ourselves better as a result of this encounter. Now we are prepared to focus our attention again on our world and our responsibilities.

Prayer is a time to reflect upon the will of God for our lives in response to his Word. Prayer is a time of tuning up, realigning our thinking with God's. True prayer is an opportunity to discern God's will and know his direction.

This discernment is based, in part, on knowing ourselves better, and self-knowledge is enhanced through *reflection on our joys and sorrows*. This may seem strange to many. What do our feelings have to do with prayer? Many of us were actually taught to deny feelings, to live above our emotions. But humans are emotional beings. Therefore, recognition of our feelings is a crucial factor in self-understanding. It is also a key means by which we can appreciate how God is working in our lives.

In a sense, this spiritual exercise involves thanksgiving, confession, and care-casting. Former generations of Christians have viewed this exercise as the examination of conscience, as a form of guilt-casting from their inner lives and behavior. But recent theologians are recognizing that though an acknowledgment of our failures needs to be part of our prayer experience, it is much more helpful to see these failures within the context of the whole emotional life.

John Carmody, for example, suggests that essentially this exercise in prayer is an act of giving attention to what we have been experiencing. We focus on the tender places—joy and sadness, which, Carmody says, are important indicators of the life of the inner person.[3] This assumes a basic honesty—a straightforward recognition of where we did well and where we fell short.

In describing this exercise, Carmody writes, "In starting to examine our consciences, we do well to fix our attention on the things that count, on the projects, persons and episodes that have left an emotional trace." It is, then, a careful and selective review of our recent past. This assumes that "God tends to move us, to want to teach us through our emotional gains and losses. He wants, as well, slowly to move us to some purchase on our emotions, some freedom from their dominance."[4]

In facing up to our joys and sorrows, we can come to grips with our responsibilities. Our assumption is that we are living far below our potential if our lives are unexamined. Self-knowledge is the basic ingredient to growth in wisdom and spiritual maturity.

In reflecting on the touchstones of our lives—our joys and sorrows—we can mature in the art of spiritual discernment. It is helpful to work with a journal and look back on our prayers, noting especially the feelings experienced in the time of silence following the meditation upon the Word. Naturally, this takes time. It takes a commitment not merely to prayer but to extended prayer—time alone with God. Reflection requires time.

Our daily prayers are vital to the discernment process, but we will often need a more extended leave from our daily responsibilities to find the spiritual space to hear God's voice.

Our time with God, as his children, should also include intercession—for our needs and the needs of others. Our Father delights to hear and respond to the needs of his children. Further, one of the pivotal means by which we serve others is through our intercession. For many Christians, prayer is equated with intercession. In stressing the need to see prayer as communion, I am not denying the place of petition in prayer. But many have found that in emphasizing communion and discernment in prayer, the time of intercession is not so long. It may well be that this development reflects a greater knowledge of God and a keener sensitivity to his will.

Finally, it is vital that our prayers conclude with a fresh commitment to the Lord. If we have confessed sin, our commitment is to turn from sin; if we have cast our cares on our Father, our commitment is to trust him more; if we have heard his call to serve him, our commitment is one of simple obedience. This includes the conscious dependence upon the grace of God for that to which he is calling us.

THE SPIRITUAL RETREAT

It would seem fair to say that a daily or regular time in prayer was a consistent part of Jesus' experience. But there is also evidence that on occasion he spent a more extended time apart from the crowds and needy people—

sometimes alone, and sometimes with his disciples. Jesus' ministry, for example, began after an extended time in retreat—forty days in the desert.

The example of Jesus is a reminder of the consistent word we hear through the writings of our spiritual forefathers and mothers—that there is significant value not only in a daily time of prayer but also in a spiritual retreat. At regular intervals in our lives, particularly at crucial turning points or decision-making times, it is valuable, if not essential, that we take an extended time to be with God. This could be a retreat of a day or several days.

Fruitful as our daily time of prayer may be, we often recognize that the intense activity and heaviness of our daily lives and responsibilities require extended time away from them. We need a renewal of perspective, a fresh sense of the love and goodness of God, and wisdom in the face of a critical decision. We often need a deepening of our experience in God.

In many respects, a spiritual retreat can follow the pattern of our daily prayers. (See a suggested format for a spiritual retreat in Appendix 2.) The same components and exercises can be used in a more extensive and thorough fashion in a retreat. But some factors could make a retreat unique, different from our daily prayers in more ways than just the length of our time with God.

Ideally, a retreat should include the element of spiritual direction. If possible, there should be an individual who can serve as a guide in our prayer lives, someone who can help us interpret our prayer experience, encourage us to persevere when we are discouraged, and serve as a codiscerner in a time of decision making. (More will be said about the possible role of a spiritual director in chapter 9.)

Also, a spiritual retreat can (in a sense different from our daily prayers) serve as an opportunity for us to grow in wisdom and spiritual discernment. At turning points in our lives, we need to seek the mind of God and allow his redeeming presence to purify our motives and clarify our vision of what God is doing in our lives.

We recognize that even with a consistent prayer life, with daily prayers that are rewarding and sustaining, we still live on the surface. For many Christians, the concerns and burdens of daily life are heavy and dominate their thinking. They will need a day or two away from their responsibilities before they can be freed of anxieties and experience an abiding peace that allows them to hear the voice of God. The busyness of our minds is not eased in a few minutes. It often takes time, extended time alone with God, before we are still enough to hear his voice and discern his perfect will for our lives.

For many of us, it is only during extended time with God that we confront the deeper questions in our lives— our deep fears and loneliness, our pride and longing for recognition and honor, our secret sins, and our lack of devotion to Christ.

The spiritual retreat, as with our daily prayers, is governed by a simple principle: We seek to know and love Christ more fully. We believe we can meet him in quietness and solitude. It is not that Christ is not everywhere present by his spirit; it is not that the Lord is to be found only in the prayer closet. No. It is simply that if we are going to meet God and hear his voice and grow in wisdom as we meet and encounter our Lord, we need first to still our hearts and minds. We need to step aside from the business of our daily responsibilities—daily, but also for a few days every few months or every year.

Finally, it is worth noting that our daily private prayers and our spiritual retreats complement our participation in public worship with the people of God. There are individual and communal dimensions to prayer, and a full Christian experience includes both.

CHAPTER 8

Vocation and Christian Service

*S*pirituality encompasses the whole of life. One of the classic, though very common, errors concerning the Christian life is the idea that the spiritual refers to the religious. Many think of their lives as having secular and sacred dimensions, and often, for them, the sacred or spiritual means their religious activities.

But true spirituality includes every aspect of life. It is as whole beings that we are children of the Father in every dimension of our lives. We are in union with Christ and walking in the Spirit every day, regardless of whether we are working, playing, praying, or sleeping. Thus, we must see our activity in the world—whether as parents and homemakers, students, businesspersons, teachers, politicians, preachers, or whatever the occupation—as a component of an authentic spirituality.

I have sought to stress how a component of a Christian spirituality needs to be incorporated into our experience. But for this component, the focus will be different. I will seek to show how this component needs to be viewed in a new perspective. We will ask a different question: How can this dimension of our lives be a component in spirituality?

In one sense, it is already a component, whether we are conscious of it or not. On the other hand, a conscious decision to make the whole of our lives spiritual, including our activity in the world, can show us how our roles in the world can foster our union with Christ. How can our roles as members of families and congregations, our occupations in the office or school, and our areas of responsibility and service be dimensions of spirituality?

RECOGNIZING GOD'S PERSONAL CALL

At least four factors determine whether our activity in the world is an integral part of spirituality. One is the recognition that our activity in the world is in response to God's personal call. Somehow each of us needs to see that the task in the world, in its various dimensions, is in fulfillment of divine call. It is vocation.

This component rests on a theological principle: God is establishing his kingdom on earth. He calls men and women to identify with this mission and equips them to be his kingdom agents in the world. This kingdom is a kingdom of peace, whose king is the Prince of Peace. In establishing his kingdom, the Lord has entrusted to his people a ministry of reconciliation. We are agents of peace, or peacemakers.

James Fowler is very helpful on the subject of vocation in his book *Becoming Adult, Becoming Christian*.[1] The book seeks to understand the question of faith and vocation within the context of developmental psychology. He stresses that a Christian understanding of vocation establishes human activity in the purposes of God. We become his partners—coworkers with the Creator-Redeemer in his task of peacemaking. Vocation, then, is not job, livelihood, or occupation. It may include this, but it is not limited to this. Vocation is not to be identified with profession or career. Profession or career may be an expression of divine calling, or vocation, but vocation is bigger than profession. Fowler writes,

> Vocation is the response a person makes with his or her total self to the address of God and to the calling to partnership. The shaping of vocation as total response of the self to the address of God involves the orchestration of our leisure, our relationships, our work, our private life, our public life, and of the resources we steward, so as to put it all at the disposal of God's purposes in the services of God and the neighbor.[2]

This view of vocation is liberating.[3] We are freed, for example, from competition with others. Each one has a unique calling or endowment that does not need to be established in competition with others. There is no fear that one's vocation will be fulfilled by others; the opportunities are vast in number. We can rejoice in and appreciate the gifts and abilities of others. Rather than envy other persons or be threatened by their abilities, we can actually and freely appreciate their contributions to us and the common good. We are not depreciated by the giftedness of others.

Fowler actually suggests that vocation is discerned in community. Consequently, one's vocation must serve the common good; this means that vocation is not so much found as it is negotiated as one carves a place within the greater community. We shape our purposes in terms of the needs and purposes of the community. We live in mutual submission and mutual trust within that community. Fowler calls this community of faith an ecology of vocations.[4]

Therefore, the first factor that determines whether our activity in the world is a component of spirituality is whether we are acting in response to God's unique call upon our lives. (Appendix 3 provides a perspective on discerning and recognizing your vocation.)

EXERCISING VOCATION WITH GENEROSITY AND HUMILITY

A second factor that determines if our activity in the world is a dimension of our spiritual lives is the extent to which we are fulfilling our vocations with generosity and humility.

We are God's servants—fulfilling our vocations in love for God and for neighbor. An authentic vocation is literally lived for others. True service is richly rewarding and is a source of deep joy for us. But our activity in the world is counterproductive if it is governed by self-gratification and self-ambition. The motive is that the activity glorifies God and helps others. We serve not with calculation but with generosity. There is a joyful abandon in our desire to fulfill God's purposes and meet real needs. We eagerly help our children, make our homes, serve our neighbors, and fulfill our daily occupations in response to God's generosity toward us. We therefore avoid calculated self-interest.

The call to humility is a call to serve God with sober minds—with full awareness of our gifts and our limitations. In discerning the call of God, we recognize that there is a corresponding endowment of ability, giftedness, and opportunity to fulfill this call. If God calls, God equips. But God has not gifted us to do everything. Neither do we have supernatural powers of mental skills and physical strength. We serve with generosity but not with foolishness. There is a gentle tension between generosity and a recognition of limitations.

This, too, is liberating. We are freed from feeling the necessity of being all things to all people. We are not messiahs; we are not failures when we cannot fulfill all expectations. In vocation we experience our limits as well as our possibilities. Our responsibility is great but not unlimited. In this respect we are freed from overextending ourselves. We can freely have an appropriate level of participation in family, education or culture, economy, government, and church. We do not have to work to vindicate our worth. And as a result, we are also freed from the tyranny of time. We are called, Fowler notes, into time, not in a battle against time.[5]

In the gospel of Mark, chapter 1 (the text referred to in chapter 7), Jesus came from his time of prayer with a clear sense of the direction he was to go. He knew his vocation clearly. Though filled with compassion, and despite the clamor of the city of Capernaum, Jesus turned from that city and went to others to fulfill his calling to preach. The actions surely would have disappointed the disciples. They would have been confused. Is this man a servant? Does he not care for the people of Capernaum? Jesus did care; he was a man of compassion. But Jesus had a calling to fulfill, and it was more important for him to be a servant than to be known as a servant. This, in part, is what it means to fulfill our vocations in humility. We cannot be all things to all people, despite our generosity. Those around us will not always understand this—but that is a small price to pay.

We cannot effectively fulfill our vocations or hear the voice of God in the course of our active and full days if we are physically, emotionally, or intellectually drained. We can safely assume that God has a vocation or a calling for each of his people. But his yoke is easy. It is easy not in that there is little work to do. His yoke is easy in that it fits us just right. His yoke will challenge and stretch us, and it will force us to depend on his grace. But frequently, we take on additional weight—extra burdens that God did not intend for us. A good principle to remember is this: Generous, willing people will always have more expectations to fulfill than they can possibly accomplish. Therefore, saying no, recognizing limitations and vocational focus, is part of true service.

Furthermore, the task to which we are called will include sacrificial service—a full identification with the Crucified One. Generosity means that it will cost us something. But there are certain elements we cannot and need not sacrifice for the kingdom. We are not called to sacrifice our time with God, our marriages, or our children. Darrell Johnson, pastor of the Glendale Presbyterian Church in Glendale, California, put it well: "God sacrificed his Son so that I would never need to sacrifice my son." This does not mean that we spend all our time in prayer or that we idolize the marriage or the family. Generous service will cost the spouse and the family, also. But an authentic God-given vocation is wholly consistent with a full marriage and family life. God *has* provided for the possibility of vocations (expressed through professions or church ministries) that involve long separations. His provision is celibacy (1 Cor. 7). Some are called to singleness for the sake of the kingdom. But persons who are married, and with children, are not free to sacrifice these life relationships for the sake of their vocations. To do so is to violate crucial dimensions of a Christian spirituality.

MEETING GOD IN THE WORLD

A third factor that determines whether our activity in the world is a component of spirituality is whether we are prepared to meet God and hear his voice in and through this activity. As parents, can we find God through our children? As businesspersons, is God in the marketplace?

Peter met God in the world. When he was called of God to meet and respond to Cornelius, he suddenly discovered that the gospel was as much for the Gentile as for himself, a Jew. He was converted! He found that the Spirit had preceded him in the world. Peter, willing to meet God in the world and hear God's voice, was turned around by what he discovered.

We cannot think of God as somehow being confined inside the walls of our churches or of our prayer closets. So frequently we tend to develop a ghetto mentality when we think of God's role in the world—that is, thinking that God is somehow *our* God, and that he is Lord of the Christian community, while the evil one is the lord of the world or of everything outside the confines of religious activity.

This is a faulty perception on two accounts. First, we cannot say that we are all on God's side because we know perfectly well that a battle wages continually in our minds. Spiritual warfare is principally a battle for the Christian mind, and the war is far from over. We are not perfect in motive. We still have much to learn; many areas of our thinking need conversion.

Second, this is a faulty perception of the world. As Peter came to discover, the Spirit was active in the world long before Peter appeared on the scene. The Scriptures confirm that God has left a witness of himself in the conscience of every person. Every person, family, and culture can bear witness to God in some way. We have the potential of learning from all the people we meet—whether believers or not. God can speak to us in many ways if we are prepared to see and listen.

I remember distinctly an experience I had as a young university student in Regina, Canada. I was a volunteer responsible for the book table that was sponsored and run by a group of Christians meeting on campus. For a few hours each week I would be there, meeting passersby, selling books, or just tending the book table. The hallway in which our table was set up included several other groups selling books, including the Marxists and the Marxist-Leninists and the Hare Krishnas and the anarchists (who, it seemed to me, always maintained the neatest book table). One day, a student I had not seen before came by and asked me for a book on economic injustice and the problem of world poverty.

"I have none," I said. Then he asked me where he could get books on the subject, and it struck me that across the hall was a table full of books addressing the very theme—but from a Marxist perspective. I was stunned, and I realized that my circle of faith and thinking had not sufficiently responded to the important problem. Ironically, it was through the Marxists that I first realized that there was something very wrong with the world economic order. Eventually, I came to find that God was very concerned about the problem, and that there is a fine body of literature from a Christian perspective that addresses it. But God used the Marxists to point it out to me—at least initially.

Part of meeting God in the world includes learning and discovery—discerning his presence ahead of us, hearing his voice even through people who do not affirm his lordship. But seeing and hearing God in the world also mean responding with openness to suffering, difficulty, and failure.

We are often of the mind that our goal in life is happiness. Many chose to follow the Christian faith because they sought happiness and believed that in Jesus they would find it. But God's purposes are bigger. He desires that we would be righteous. Christ's objective, as the ascended Lord of the church, is to present each of us spotless before the Father—that through the Word, we would be made whole (Eph. 5:25–27). Thus, Christ tests our faith, allows us to be tempted, permits the evil one to stretch us to the edge of our limits (but no more), which is not necessarily happiness. Through stress and distress, God is near; we find our Lord and hear his voice in the long, easy stretches as well as the more difficult roads.

If we are not prepared to see and know God in the world, we will not be freed to grow in holiness. But if we regard every personal encounter, every obstacle in our path, and every difficulty as a further means by which we can hear God's voice and experience his grace, the largest part of our waking hours (our vocations in the world) will foster spiritual vitality.

SUCCESS AND CHRISTIAN VOCATION

If God calls and equips us to fulfill a calling, can we not be confident that we will know success? No, not necessarily. Even if God did guarantee our success, what is success from God's perspective? These are crucial questions as we reflect on a Christian understanding of work and vocation. Our service, our activity in the world, cannot be a component of spirituality unless we evaluate and measure success on God's terms rather than cultural ones. This is a fourth factor that determines the extent to which a task in the world is a component of a Christian spirituality.

To start with, we need to remember that God delights in working through human notions of failure, weakness, and vulnerability. We have no guarantee of visible, outward success. God has called us to be faithful in fulfilling the task he has given to each of us, and often the most significant work that he will accomplish will be through what is perceived in the world as failure. But it seems fair to say that if God calls and equips us for a task, he usually expects to fulfill his purposes through us as we accomplish that task—as we are successful in completing the responsibilities he has given to us. But we need to rethink our notions of success.

We can identify four characteristics of a biblical understanding of success. First, success in the kingdom of God is a relative matter. We tend to evaluate all people on an equal basis and by a standard measurement. In a school, some students receive good grades and some poor grades. In some cases, grades reflect the student's discipline and commitment, but they also are evidence of intelligence and ability. The grading system is not wrong in itself, but it does not necessarily reflect kingdom values. In God's kingdom, some have received five talents, another ten talents, and others only one talent. And the freedom we have is that we are evaluated accordingly.

This could be understood more broadly. We are responsible, and are judged successful by God, to the extent that we have been faithful stewards of the abilities, gifts, resources, and opportunities we have. We are evaluated individually—and in the end, only God can make a fair statement of our success or failure. Only God can see the whole picture.

Second, in the kingdom of God, there is no success in the Christian community at the expense of others. We are all winners or all losers. Competition in terms of numbers, influence, and status is incompatible with kingdom values. God's calling and God's vision are unique to individuals and organizations, but they are also complementary to other vocations and visions.

Third, in the kingdom, success is not the only or even the highest ideal. We are not committed to success at any expense. A commitment to an ideal or a vision of success can blind us to other priorities and other kinds of work that God is doing. God can and often does some of his most remarkable work through our failures. When we are weak, he often has the means by which to display his strength and glory. But even when we do have valid ideals, our success will be a false one if we compromise ourselves or our vocations in the pursuit of these goals. Success is not the highest value in the kingdom.

Finally, for God, bigger is not necessarily better. In 1985, there was a massive multicity global broadcast of a seminar/conference for young people. Manila, Philippines, where I used to live, was one of the sites for the simultaneous program. I will never forget the sense of awe that struck people at the thought of such a massive production. We tend to be impressed by technological wizardry on such a grand scale. But this is not the case with God. God values holiness, faith, love, and good works. He sees significance and eternal worth in what may be very small in our eyes. Jesus, for example, saw meaning in the two coins of the widow in contrast to the more impressive giving of others. In the kingdom, the widow's two small coins meant far more.

We tend to be impressed by big churches, big programs, and confident personalities who have education, great speaking or musical abilities, and wealth. But God sees things differently, and if we are to find success and foster union with Christ through our activity in the world, we need to be aligned with his perspective.

CHAPTER 9

Spiritual Authority and Accountability

THE NEED FOR ACCOUNTABILITY

*I*gnatius Loyola spoke of a willingness to call what is black white and what is white black if it were so directed or decreed by the church. Protestants usually respond to this idea with horror and indignation. For a Protestant, black would be white and white black only if there were chapter and verse in Holy Writ that indicated as much. But though Protestants and many contemporary Catholics recoil from the hierarchicalism of Ignatius and his apparent unthinking subservience, a closer look reveals that he was affirming a cardinal principle of the spiritual life—submission to authority. We may not appreciate the way the principle was expressed, but spiritual submission is an essential component of a Christian spirituality. The vow of obedience that characterized the spiritual life of Ignatius was unique, but the principle of accountability is a universal one for the Christian community.

A Protestant Concern

Cults are easily possible among Protestants for the simple reason that individual teachers or preachers with questionable doctrinal foundations can suddenly and freely start a movement, and no one has the prerogative or right to call them to accountability.

This is perhaps *the* component of Christian spirituality that is most lacking among contemporary Protestants. The Reformation affirmed the right of individuals to hear the voice of God, to worship God through Christ without the mediation of a priest, and to understand the Scriptures in their own language. But individualism, while affirming valid biblical truths, had the unfortunate tendency of undercutting other equally valid truths—specifically the principle of spiritual authority and accountability. Christians somehow came up with the idea that they are autonomous and stand alone before God with no direct accountability to the church or the authority of church leaders. But the weight of the scriptural evidence strongly supports the principle of authority and accountability. The lack of this component represents a spiritually dangerous state of affairs.

Many Christians live as spiritual hermits. Our interior lives are secret worlds known only to ourselves. In some cases the dark corners of our lives are unknown to us because we fail to live up to them and face them honestly and courageously. In part we are afraid of these dark shadows of the soul. As Protestants, we tend to live alone as spiritual hermits—confessing to no one, acknowledging little of what happens in the inner world, and experiencing little spiritual friendship—that of having someone who represents any degree of spiritual authority in our lives. We lack structures of spiritual accountability.

Yet the words of Scripture affirm again and again that no one stands alone before God. Even the apostles were accountable to one another, as evidenced by the Jerusalem Council. The apostle Paul speaks of the need for mutual submission, of obedience to people assigned to spiritual leadership—whether they be pastors, elders, or bishops.

Spiritual Obedience

Spiritual obedience is one of the marks of the church. In Scripture, we are called to confess our sins to one another and to live in mutual submission, humbling ourselves before one another within the Christian community. Though the move away from this dimension of the spiritual life can be traced to the Protestant Reformation, the Reformers themselves, and John Wesley after them, cannot be faulted for failing to call for accountability. Each of them acknowledged the priesthood of all believers but also stressed the principle of spiritual authority within the church. Wesley is well known for the intense small group meetings that characterized the Methodist movement. There were no Wesleyan individualists. To be part of the movement of spiritual renewal meant that one was actively involved as a member of a band or a class group that met for mutual accountability and ministry.

Somehow, we need to recognize the need for accountability and express it concretely if our spiritual lives are to have stability and continual growth. We are not spiritual nomads; authentic Christianity cannot be lived in isolation as an interior hermit. David Augsburger notes the importance of this for all Christians, but he places particular stress on people in leadership positions. He warns that public ministry is in constant danger of destroying the leader if appropriate channels of accountability are not in place. He validly insists that mutual accountability and interdependence are essential to overcome the individualism of Western Christianity. Augsburger suggests that our egalitarian society has, in part, led us to abandon vertical models of authority. But they have not been replaced with models of mutual accountability and community.[1]

We tend to think of authority figures as people who make our lives unpleasant or put limits on our joy and freedom. But in actual fact, living under identifiable authority grants us both perspective and freedom. I am a squash player who enjoys playing as well as thinking about the game. In squash, in contrast to tennis, the player who wins is usually the one who is able to control the center of the court. When I was receiving instruction, the trainer kept insisting that after every shot, I needed to return quickly and as effortlessly as possible to the center of the court. From there I could with two strides return just about any shot from my opponent. When I lost a point, it was usually because I was caught off center.

In the same way, authority in our lives is like a central point of reference—something that we can come back to again and again to give us perspective and prepare us for just about anything that comes our way. Without structures of authority, we are less likely to have our bearings and be well situated to respond to what comes up in our lives. The squash player who controls the center actually has more freedom to respond, not less, because of the restraints that come with returning to the center after every stroke.

ESTABLISHING STRUCTURES AND PATTERNS OF ACCOUNTABILITY

We need to acknowledge the dangers of spiritual isolation, but we also need to activate potential structures for living in submission to others. The authority of Christ's lordship over our lives can and will be expressed through a variety of ministries.

The Pastor

First, it is essential that we live in submission to the preached Word and the administered sacrament. We Christians cannot know spiritual vitality unless we know the power of spiritual preaching and the nourishment of the spiritual food of the Lord's Table. Yet these have meaning only if we live in submission to the one that God has placed in the ministry as preacher and pastor. We need to consciously recognize, during each worship event, that Christ is speaking to us and feeding us, in the Word and sacrament, through a person, a fellow human being. Christ can minister to us only if we worship him in submission to his appointed servant.

Mutual Submission

Second, authentic Christian life includes full congregational life. We are part of a Christian community, and community is impossible without submission. Each community has elders or comparable individuals who are the recognized spiritual leaders of the assembly. They have spiritual authority; the congregation as a whole lives in mutual submission. No one stands alone, not even the pastor/preacher. All are called to live in community.

The Small Group and the Spiritual Director

Third, we need a pattern of accountability that is more intentional and defined. There are two options—one very much a part of the Protestant spiritual heritage, the other more common within Catholicism. Both are models that can effectively break down the barrier of isolation that characterizes the inner lives of so many Christian believers. One model is the small group; the other is the spiritual director or friend.

Many Christians find it valuable to be part of a small group that serves as a close community of peers. These groups can take various forms, but ideally, the group should meet regularly, every week or two weeks, for reflection on the Scriptures, sharing of personal concerns (including areas of failure), encouragement and counsel between the participants, and prayer. Many times, leaders within congregational life are involved in small group ministries but, usually, in a pastoral or study leader capacity. The genius of these groups is that the leader is only a facilitator or coordinator of the time together. It is a gathering of peers, who exercise mutual accountability and mutual ministry.

Protestants also are rediscovering the vital place of a spiritual friend and director—something that Roman

Catholics have known of for centuries. A spiritual friend or director (I will use the terms interchangeably for the moment) is an individual with whom you openly discuss and reflect on the inner pilgrimage of your life. In the presence of that individual, the inner recesses of your mind and heart are no longer so secret. In a formal relationship, the heart of spiritual direction is the act of guiding the prayer life of a fellow pilgrim; informally, a spiritual friend is a fellow pilgrim you trust for guidance, encouragement, and counsel and with whom you feel sufficiently accepted so that you are free to confess your sins.

Alan Jones cited two reasons why it is profitable for Christians to have a spiritual director;[2] I will add a third. These reasons apply also to the value of a small group. We need a spiritual director/friend because of our capacity for self-deception. People who acknowledge a need for spiritual direction and friendship have no illusions about their spiritual maturity and strength. This recognition arises out of genuine humility. The heart is deceptively wicked. Our motives are far from pure, however much we might wish they were sanctified. We need a friend, a director, who can ask us the questions we may well be avoiding.

The friends who love us most do so unreservedly but also with discrimination. They do not love blindly or foolishly. The book of Proverbs includes many descriptions of genuine friendship. We note in Proverbs 27:6 (NIV) that a true friend is characterized by candor: A false friend flatters, but "faithful are the wounds of a friend" (note also Prov. 28:23). In other words, spiritual friendship includes a willingness to confront, to challenge motives, actions, and priorities. We enter willingly into this kind of relationship because of our capacity for self-deception. Each of us needs the honesty of a true friend. We need to know, without doubt, that there is someone who is candid with us.

A spiritual director and/or friend is also of great value because of our constant need for hope. Our tasks in the world are filled with obstacles and difficulties. We have vocations, but we seem to encounter failure and frustration at every turn. We lose hope; our courage wanes. We all need encouragement—someone to restore our hope. But encouragement is empty language when it is not accompanied by love. Our hope is restored when we are reassured and reminded of God's grace and work while confident of love and acceptance. We must not underestimate the transforming power of divine love working through a director or friend. We all need this love, expressed through reassuring words, that restores our hope, renews our vision, and reestablishes our confidence in God. And we need it constantly.

Then also, we need a spiritual director and/or friend to serve as a codiscerner when we are making important decisions in our lives. This includes questioning motives with candor and honesty. It includes giving encouragement so that by divine grace we can fulfill God's call for us. But more specifically, we need someone to help us listen to God's voice when we come to a fork in the road. A spiritual director can assist by helping us discern our feelings and motives during prayer; a friend can hear us and help weigh pros and cons of the choices we face. By direction, I do not mean that the person will be the Spirit to us or tell us what to do. No. A spiritual director or friend does not replace the guidance of the Holy Spirit. Rather, a spiritual director can serve as a codiscerner—helping us hear the voice of the Lord clearly and encouraging us to respond wholeheartedly.

Thomas Green, in his book *Come Down Zacchaeus*, has suggested that we should look for four qualities in choosing a spiritual director:[3] First, we should be comfortable with the person; second, the person should understand what we are seeking in prayer and spirituality; third, the person should be able to respond objectively in interpreting our personal experience in prayer; and fourth, the person should ideally be someone we recognize as being ahead of us in the spiritual pilgrimage. As Green notes, good directors are hard to find. But his reminder is well taken. God is committed to our spiritual growth. He will not leave us alone. By his grace, we can find an individual who can direct our spiritual experience.

The spiritual director and/or friend is an important person in our circle of accountability, probably playing the critical role. But our humanity as men and women of community needs to be expressed and fulfilled in a wide range of relationships. We are not hermits, however quiet or retiring our personality styles may be. Authentic spirituality is lived in community. Some of the most outgoing people are lonely on the inside; they sometimes have few intimate and intentional personal relationships.

I would suggest that each adult should have about twenty meaningful relationships. Each of us needs at least twenty individuals who play a significant role in the family, workplace, church, neighborhood, and circle of friends. These are mutual and reciprocal relationships—consisting of friends (probably no more than three or four) and acquaintances who know us well. This network of relationships is essential for a healthy emotional, psychological, and spiritual life. These persons, though not all may be believers, represent another dimension of the authority of Christ in our lives.

So far I have suggested three ways in which we can acknowledge spiritual authority and live in spiritual accountability: submission to the preached Word, mutual submission within a congregation of Christian believers, and an intentional relationship of submission within a small group of believers and/or to a spiritual director and friend. There is a fourth means by which we can concretely express this principle. Spiritual accountability can be exercised through spiritual reading—the careful, meditative reading of the devotional or spiritual classics.

This reading is designed to increase not merely knowledge about God but personal intimate knowledge of God. It is valuable to read the spiritual classics as literature, reflecting on the piety of another age in the history of the church. But spiritual reading is different, for it arises out of our conviction that within the universal church God has gifted some individuals to express remarkably, for all ages, the nature of the spiritual life and what A. W. Tozer calls "the deep things of God." We view these authors not as ancient historical figures but as pastors and teachers to Christians even today. Martin Luther still serves as a pastor through his writings;

Bernard of Clairvaux still serves as a director of the spiritual life through his *On the Love of God*.

Spiritual reading is done with an open spirit, a submissive mind, and a willingness to hear God's voice and follow him. We cannot be academic and detached. We read in an attitude of accountability to the pastors and teachers of the greater Christian community, opening our lives to their penetrating words. (See Appendix 4 for a list of recommended devotional classics and a suggested approach to reading them.)

All these various forms of finding and living in accountability are just suggestions, not the only means by which we can live in community. But whether we follow these actual suggestions or not, we need to intentionally design structures of spiritual authority and accountability that will provide us with counsel, encouragement, and direction.

THE DANGER OF AUTHORITARIANISM AND SPIRITUAL DEPENDENCE

There is an attendant danger to this fourth component of a Christian spirituality—authoritarianism and spiritual dependence. Alan Jones, in his work *Exploring Spiritual Direction*, notes that spiritual direction lends itself to abuse. People long for authority figures; cults are built around strong religious, authoritarian models. Since spiritual direction is based on submission and obedience, exploitation is very possible and can be a constant temptation. People seek guidance; they are sheep seeking a shepherd. And often there will be men and women who are quite prepared to exploit the needs and vulnerability of people seeking help. Often the very people seeking guidance and counsel are not discriminating in their search for direction and spiritual friendship. Spiritual direction needs to be restored certainly, but as Jones insists, there are pitfalls to avoid.[4]

Some teachers and writers today have so emphasized authority and accountability that individual responsibility is forsaken. In calling for spiritual authority and accountability, this aspect of the spiritual life is described as absolute, so that human authority—whether parents, employers, pastors, or government leaders—is regarded as deserving complete and unquestioned obedience. This emphasis perverts an otherwise essential and good component of the Christian life.

The reason is simple. All human authority is conditional, not absolute. Ultimate authority belongs only to God. Even parents need to recognize that authentic parenting basically consists of leading children to mature responsibility for their lives under the authority of God. Government officials who undermine justice and pastors who fail to preach the Word or administer the Lord's Supper can surely be questioned by the discerning Christian. Blind submission is irresponsible.

People in positions of spiritual authority, whether as parents, pastors/elders, or spiritual directors, need to appreciate that their role is to serve Christ. A preacher should be able to confidently say to the congregation, "If you don't find it in the Scriptures, don't take it from me." True preaching leads people to the Word, not to the preacher. Elders within a congregation are called by God not to lord it over their flock but to be examples. Spiritual directors are not leading blind followers; they serve as catalysts to spiritual maturity and depth. They are midwives of the spiritual life.

Therefore, true spiritual direction can eventually lead to spiritual friendship between director and directee because what is sought is interdependence, not dependence. False spiritual authority encourages dependence; true spiritual authority fosters maturity in people, enabling them to become responsible, contributing members of a body of believers. A true counseling ministry does not create dependence; rather, it provides individuals with the mental, emotional, and spiritual tools to mature in Christ as members of a community.

This is often difficult for Christians to handle. Some prefer to remain in a position of dependence. As a father, for example, I sometimes need to push my two sons a little further than they would care to go; otherwise, they will not mature. They need to move from dependence on me to interdependence and dependence on their heavenly Father.

In the group prayer retreats I lead, the prayer times are designed to be personal encounters with Christ. Real and profound needs of the retreatants are often brought to the surface; they are anxious for help as they discern the word of the Lord. Although there to help, I have a simple rule—I will meet with the retreatants for only a few minutes at a time. It may seem much too short to the needy retreatant, but the time is long enough. After the retreat, there will be time to talk. But during the retreat, the goal is for the participants to spend time with Christ.

Figuratively speaking, I seek to throw them back in Christ's arms where they ultimately belong, and where they will need to go on their own if they are to mature in their faith. We all need spiritual direction and friendship. But this must ultimately lead to a deeper spiritual maturity and a closer relationship with Christ himself.

CHAPTER 10
Play

THE CALL TO RECREATION

*P*lay! I'm sure that at this point some readers will be asking whether this book is really about spirituality! It is. Spirituality encompasses the whole of our lives as they are lived under God. Leisure, in various forms, is part of every whole and balanced life. It, too, of necessity must be a component of spirituality. Somehow we need to see leisure and recreation as under the grace of God and, therefore, as contributing an essential element to spirituality.

The Principle of Sabbath Rest

But recreation or play does not merely become a component of spirituality because we are already engaged in it and must somehow include it. The theological basis for play is actually found in the principle of the sabbath rest. God created the earth in six days, and on the seventh he rested. Then God ordained that the Hebrew week was to be a rhythm of six and one, including work, certainly, but also including rest, a day in which work was prohibited.

For many people, the principle of sabbath rest has come to mean a day of religious activities; the more religion, the better. As children, many of us came to hate Sundays because we were taught it was a day in which we were to do religious things, notably going to public services. To complement that, we were taught that Sunday was to be not a day of recreation but a day of rest. But more and more Christians are realizing what Jesus meant when he said the Sabbath was made for people and not people for the Sabbath. The Sabbath is as much a day we reserve for ourselves as it is a day we reserve for God. Certainly, we need one day in seven in which we gather with God's people for worship and ministry. But we need one day in seven for rest, renewal, and recreation just as much. It is a day to cease from our labors as we enjoy the fruit of God's work and ours—delighting in our families, friends, homes, and neighborhoods as well as delighting in God.

Observance of sabbath rest is grounded in the conviction that there is more to life than our work. God has given us work to do—to glorify him and sustain our lives and those of our dependents. But life is not all work. In withdrawing consistently and regularly from our work, we declare that we are more than our work, and that our identity and provision lie finally in God and not in the fruit of our hands.

Living with Hope

But there is more to the theological foundation of play than just the principle of sabbath rest. Through leisure and recreation, we proclaim with our actions that we are a people of hope. There is no doubt that the world is broken; every day the newspaper reminds us of the depth of the human predicament. If we play, if we take time for friends, hobbies, sports, and the arts, it is *not* because we overlook the severity of human need. Rather, our play or recreation is rooted in our hope—our conviction that there is more to reality than meets the eye. We believe that Christ is on the throne of the universe, and that because of a victory already accomplished over evil, Christ will make all things well in his time. Our times of rest and recreation are a profound nonverbal proclamation of this hope.

I served as a pastor for several years for a small congregation in central Ontario, Canada. One evening, we were holding a church board meeting while a storm was raging outdoors. The longer we debated, the more it snowed. And unfortunately, we discussed and debated long into the evening. I lived twenty miles out of the city, and I was eager to get home to my family. When the meeting finally ended, I was soon in my car and on my way home. In my hurry, I chose to take an alternate shorter route. But with the heavy snowfall, I should have kept to the main highway. Yet I thought if I could just keep the car moving, I would not get caught up in the snowdrifts.

Well, the farther I got down that back road, the higher the drifts seemed to be. Just when I was thinking that I might make it through, I came on a very high snowdrift and plowed in before I had a chance to stop. And there I was, miles from help, sitting in a car that was stalled on a cold, stormy night.

Well, I was young and hearty, so I jumped out with the shovel in hand that I had for such occasions. And I attacked the snow with the thought that it would be but a few minutes before I was on my way. But the drift was much too large, and after fifteen minutes I knew that I had no hope of digging my way out. I began to look up and down the road, hoping that some heavenly tow truck would appear. But naturally, no one was on that road in that kind of weather!

So I had no choice but to close up the car and head off on foot. To my surprise, over the very next hill I saw a light, and soon I came upon a farmhouse. I knocked at the door, asked to use the phone, called my friend, and received immediate assurance that he was on his way. It happened that quickly. He assured me that he would be there in about twenty minutes.

I returned to the car, sat on the hood, and took in the evening. It was, and still is for me, the most beautiful winter evening I have ever experienced. The storm was over. The moon was high by then. In the quiet I saw motion to one side and turned in time to see a rabbit scurry away. A quiet hush ruled the valley, and though I was alone, I was at peace.

Before I left for the farmhouse, I was desperately hoping that help would come along that road. But after the phone call, I had hope. I *knew* that my friend was coming. And that hope gave me a powerful serenity that enabled me to see the beauty of a winter night and enjoy the quiet that comes after a storm.

As Christians, this is what we mean by hope—a confidence regarding the future that gives us peace in the present. And each time we stop our work, enjoy our world and our friends, we are reminded of that hope. Our play, then, gives perspective to the whole of our lives.

The Need to Rest

But there is yet another reason for recreation. We need rest. As people who love Christ and long to serve him wholeheartedly, we easily become overextended in our daily responsibilities. Many work seven days a week on the pretext that their vocation, specific role, or responsibility demands relentless attention. But the truth is, no one is indispensable. In failing to rest and withdraw from our work or ministry, we are essentially saying that we are somehow irreplaceable. The consequence is often a life that loses its compassionate edge and, eventually, its personal dimension. We become exhausted or burned out fulfilling a God-given vocation. We need not be impressed by people who say they work seven days a week. It would be more appropriate for us to express our concern or perhaps a word of caution. We all need to withdraw periodically, to rest and enjoy the fruit of God's work. In so doing we live in joyful anticipation of our ultimate sabbath rest, which will come with the consummation of Christ's kingdom.

Actually, the principle of sabbath rest involves much more than merely one day a week. It refers to the whole dimension of our lives that we live in simple childlike joy under God's mercy as his redeemed people. We rest from our vocations at some point every day, not just one day a week; we delight in God's created order and his gifts to us—every day, not just one day in seven.

But many Christians need to learn to play. They have consciences that frequently leave them guilty, hesitant, and inhibited because they feel play is a questionable activity. They have grown up with a work ethic that assumes all redeemed time is devoted to work. They may need to learn how to play because for too long they have simply neglected this fundamental dimension of a full Christian life. There are at least three means by which play can be incorporated and affirmed within spirituality.

HOBBIES, MUSIC AND THE ARTS, AND PLAY

The Value of a Hobby

First, the component of play in spirituality could include developing a hobby. A hobby can be defined as any regular activity having no intrinsic worth in itself other than its affirmation of beauty and order. For individuals whose vocations place them under severe stress and frustration, a retreat into a hobby may well be one of the most essential elements that maintains sound mental health and hope in their calling.

Engaging in a hobby becomes an act of faith—a regular, consistent means of declaring that beauty and order will prevail, though most of the evidence indicates otherwise. Through a hobby, whether stamp collecting, woodworking, or playing a musical instrument, we are further declaring that there is more to life than our work.

We step back and delight in one aspect of the created order that has captured the imagination—some aspect of creation or culture that affirms beauty and order and fascinates us, regardless of what others think of it.

Music and the Arts

Second, this component of spirituality could include participation in music and/or the arts. More than any other dimension of culture, it is in music and the arts that we have the privilege of responding most fully to our identity as bearers of the image of God. Some would suggest that with discipline, any person can learn to play a musical instrument and develop proficiency in one of the arts—be it painting, drama, or a handicraft.

In leaving behind our occupations and labors in the world, we are freed to step into another world—of fine music, visual arts, handicrafts, and drama. We are freed to enjoy culture and to carry out the biblical mandate to have dominion over the earth and all that is in it. In a real sense, participation in music and the arts is a continual validation of the nature of our hope. We live out our hope; we do not merely work toward it. Our delight in music and/or the arts is but one way of affirming, by faith, that the union of heaven and earth will consummate history and that ultimate reality lies in that consummation.

The Sheer Fun of It!

Third, we need to play—just for the fun of it. Physical recreation, with children and friends, is also a profound means of declaring that we do not save ourselves and that our "useful" labors are not our means of redemption. In play, we affirm that our hope rests not in our labors but in God. We are freed to leave our labors behind for a time and delight in God, his creation, and one another.

FRIENDSHIP

Play can be incorporated into our lives in various ways, and I have suggested some so far in this chapter. Play can have a private (possibly in the pursuit of a hobby) as well as a community dimension (perhaps in play or participation in the arts). But it may well be that the most crucial way play is incorporated into a Christian spirituality is in the development of authentic friendships. True spirituality includes time with friends. By this, I mean time in intimate association with peers—time that is fun, enjoyable, and rewarding because of the sheer joy of human company.

The Importance of Friendship

But true friendship is difficult to find. Many colleagues have little to talk about other than the concerns of their offices. It does not take long to realize that true friends are rare, and that false friends are present in abundance. There are those who are "friends" as long as they can get something from you. They are really seeking a customer; all they want is to sell you something. Sometimes, you sense or know that this "friend" actually wants a financial contribution toward an organization. At other times, people want to ask for a favor or a contact so they can land a job. Selling a product in the context of a friendly conversation, soliciting an endorsement or funds for a worthy cause, and seeking help for a job are not wrong in themselves. But they are wrong if people involved abuse the precious gift of friendship by acting or assuming that they are authentic friends. True friendship is rare.

Friendship is the foundational relationship of life. All other relationships are passing and temporal; friendships have the possibility of being eternal. Parent-child, teacher-student, pastor-parishioner, and employer-employee are passing relationships. These become lasting and eternal relationships when friendships develop— when a husband and a wife are friends as well as spouses, when children mature to the point that they are friends with their parents and relate to them as brothers and sisters in Christ, when colleagues enjoy one another as persons and not merely as coworkers. C. S. Lewis stated it well: "Friendship seemed the happiest and most fully human of all loves, the crown of life and the school of virtue."[1] Friendships take time to develop and are not meant to be useful in themselves. They are a foretaste of heaven; they are relationships in which people are enjoyed and appreciated merely because they are friends.

True spiritual maturity includes the development of friendships—men and women in whose company there are mutual acceptance, love, and encouragement. Without apology, we need to recognize that in this life we will have few such friends. We may have many acquaintances, but the demands of intimate friendship are such that each individual will have few, possibly no more than six, at any given period. Then again without apology, we need to take time to be with friends for a meal together, an outing, or a time of conversation.

The point is that friendships will not happen naturally. They must be intentionally cultivated. This is due in part to the fact that, as James Olthius notes, friendship is the least necessary relation.[2] We have natural or instinctual commitments in marriage and family. We need to work and be part of a governed society. We need education. But we think we can get by without friends—intimate associations of mutual acceptance, reciprocity, and encouragement.

But friendship is the foundational relationship of life. Without it, life is a wilderness; in friendship, we experience one of the most profound gifts from God.

The Meaning of Friendship

It would be helpful perhaps to indicate what it means to be a friend. Friendship is characterized, first, by equality. Friends are peers who freely choose to associate with each other. In friendship, there is no superior, boss, or teacher. Some people do not know how to relate as a peer and, therefore, are immediately lost. Thus, learning to relate to people in a spirit of mutuality is part of learning to be a friend and receive friendship.

Second, friends are drawn to each other by something they hold in common that leads to camaraderie, or what Olthius calls congeniality.[3] It could be a common task or goal, a common concern or conviction, or some other mutual interest. But congeniality is more difficult to define. It is that unique something, that mysterious quality that draws persons to each other, often with an apparent lack of common interests. There is a strange and unique bonding of personalities.

But equality and congeniality are not the most important or most essential factors in a friendship, for friendship can cross cultural barriers, age differences, and many other apparent obstacles. The heart of friendship is commitment that is expressed in mutual acceptance, mutual appreciation, and mutual affirmation. The black mark of friendship is treachery or broken trust; its hallmark is loyalty. By definition, this commitment leaves others out. It is a commitment that gives preference, special attention, and unique trust. Friends choose to support each other, depend on each other, and enjoy each other. As such, friends are perhaps the most tangible evidence of love other than that experienced in a healthy marriage. It is a gift from God—to be received with gratitude and cultivated carefully. Friendship is worth the investment of our time and energies.

Cross-Gender Friendship

One obvious issue is friendship with members of the opposite sex. Paul exhorted Timothy to treat an older man as if he were his own father. Likewise, Timothy was to speak "to younger men as brothers, to older women as mothers, to younger women as sisters—with absolute purity" (1 Tim. 5:1–2). Timothy was given the freedom and encouragement to relate to women as his peers and friends, as though they were his sisters.

Friendship includes physical contact, but physical contact does not mean a sexual relationship, any more than it does when a son embraces his mother. Friendships with the opposite sex need not threaten a marriage. A marriage is based not on desire or physical attraction but on trust and commitment. Thus, friendships with persons of the same or opposite sex can strengthen and support our marriages.

If a friendship leads to intense physical desire, it needs to be broken. True friendship respects the commitments and associations we have made; a true sister respects her brother's marriage, and vice versa. If this trust is violated, the friendship will have to end. But this does not need to be the case. It *is* possible for men to treat younger women as sisters in all purity and for women to treat men as brothers in all purity. The paramount example of such friendships is of Jesus himself with two women very dear to him. Mary and Martha were special in his life. Very simply, the two women were his friends—sisters, whom he treated with all purity.

Jesus told his disciples that he would no longer call them servants but friends (John 15:15). He indicated that they had entered into a unique relationship with him, a relationship made for heaven. As followers of Jesus, we, too, have the privilege to call a fellow man or woman a friend. And when we do, we are going beyond the limits of our temporal, necessary, or natural relationships. We step into another time zone, another sphere of life. We have the power and the freedom to choose to give and receive friendship and live in trust and commitment and reciprocal acceptance, appreciation, and affirmation. And when we do, we have a foretaste of heaven.

Play, as the fifth component of spirituality, will probably take the least of our time. But that does not make play less essential or less important. We need to make time (say no to the extended demands of our occupations and even sometimes of the church) and regularly find refreshment and quiet with our friends, our hobbies, and the arts. Some individuals perhaps need to limit their leisure activities if this component has become their reason for living to the neglect of the Christian community, the vocation, and the renewing of the mind. This imbalance, though, is not solved by the rejection of leisure or play. A well-rounded spirituality will include a rhythm of work, rest, play, and prayer. When the rhythm is disturbed, our spiritual lives suffer, whether the disruption occurs in our occupations or our leisure.

EPILOGUE

A Call to Routine and Rhythm

Our lives are living confessions of the peace of God when they are characterized by order. An orderly life does not preclude freedom and spontaneity. It merely affirms that there is no freedom without form; there is no spontaneity without structure. Part of the beauty of the monastic tradition was the simplicity and consistency of the routine and rhythms of daily life for the monks. It would seem appropriate that we, too, should strive for order—routine and rhythm—in our experience.

First, there is the order of a rhythm between solitude and community. A full Christian experience includes solitude—for study, prayer, and even elements of play—complemented by community—again, for study, prayer, service, and play. There is a balance between the individual and personal dimensions of spirituality and the dimensions we live as part of a community of like-minded believers.

Each of the five essential components of an authentic spirituality should have an individual as well as a corporate expression. We study alone; we study in community. We know the prayer of solitude; we participate in the public worship of the people of God. We have learned to work alone in the service of God; we also have developed the ability to work with others. We have individual lines of accountability—a spiritual director or friend; we are also potentially a part of a small group of peers for encouragement and accountability. And we have a hobby and the freedom to spend time alone; we have learned the joy of friendships and recreation with others. The spiritual life includes both dimensions—the individual and the community.

Second, there is the order of routine in our daily lives. This does not imply adherence to strict legalistic rules. But we are creatures of habit, and we function best in routine. The five components do not need to be part of each day, and we will certainly not have equal amounts of each component. But the freedom of routine is still possible. A week, for example, could be a routine of six and one, of active fulfillment of our responsibilities in the world matched by a day of recreation. A day may include prayer, work, and recreation, which we live out in a consistent and orderly fashion. And the evident order of our lives assures that each of the essential components of a Christian spirituality is truly integrated into our experience.

Order—routine and rhythm—is by itself a discipline that confers a balance among the various components and between the individual and community aspects of spirituality.

APPENDIX 1

A Suggested Format for Daily Prayers

The following suggested format could be adapted to individual preferences or the needs of a particular day or prayer hour.

Focus

Center your thoughts on God; allow your mind to be stilled by the Spirit. Read a psalm or sing a hymn.

Reading of Scripture

Read and meditate on a text of Scripture. This is different from study. Ideally, it should be a passage that is known to you so that questions of interpretation are already resolved. Make it a consecutive reading—with each prayer time, stay with the same text, or move on to the text within the same book of the Bible.

Allow the Word to settle more deeply in your consciousness; permit the Word to feed your soul and be a window to God and his purposes. Read, reread, and read slowly.

Contemplate Christ as revealed in Scripture (particularly if the text used is from the Gospels); reflect on the implications of the Word for your life and work.

Silence

You are in the presence of God. Be silent if only for five minutes. Remember, words can get in the way of prayer if you are prone to babbling. As the mind is distracted, gently but firmly turn back to an awareness of the presence of God.

Then in response to the word of Scripture, following a time of silence, do any one of the following:

- Adoration/worship. Make a conscious, verbal affirmation of the goodness and glory of God.
- Thanksgiving. Call to mind God's goodness and mercy.
- Confession. Acknowledge failures and shortcomings before the Lord; seek forgiveness.
- Care-casting. Identify your fears and worries—and cast these cares upon your heavenly Father.

Each of these four (adoration, thanksgiving, confession, and care-casting) could be part of daily prayers, but one or the other will be more appropriate at different times. These four exercises could also be found at the beginning of prayers on occasions when this seems appropriate.

Discernment

Reflect on the joys and sorrows of the past day; identify where the Lord is seeking to make an impression on your conscience. Note particularly the thoughts that arose during the time of silence following the meditation on Scripture.

Intercession

Pray that God's will would be done on earth; pray for colleagues, family, friends, and others (including enemies), that they would know the wisdom and strength of God. Reflect on the challenges, problems, and opportunities you face, and ask for divine assistance. He is ready to help in time of need.

Renewed Commitment

Renew your resolve to live according to the purposes of God in obedience to his Word and by his grace.

If there has been a word of direction or guidance discerned during the hour of prayer, respond with willingness to do God's will, a commitment of intent to live by his grace under his Word.

It is also helpful to begin and end the prayer time with a hymn.

APPENDIX 2

A Suggested Format for a Spiritual Retreat★

In some respects, a retreat is merely an extension and expansion of daily prayers. But with more time, you can respond more deliberately to the presence of God and his Word. It is helpful to approach a day of prayer or a spiritual retreat well prepared. Have a plan. It is also good to set a purpose from the beginning. Will your retreat be an extended prayer time with God, or are you seeking a word of direction or guidance from the Lord? Take the following resources for the retreat:

- A Bible in a contemporary translation
- A hymnbook with an extended section of classic hymns of praise and adoration
- A notebook to serve as a journal
- On longer retreats, a devotional classic (see Appendix 3)

Think in terms of forty-five- to sixty-minute prayer periods. For each period, follow the basic format of daily prayers as suggested in Appendix 1. Sing a hymn; focus on God; reflect on appropriate Scripture for the theme of the day or the phase of the retreat. Conclude each prayer period with a few comments in your journal, describing your impressions, addressing God and telling him what is happening in prayer and what you hear him saying.

★The format suggested is an adaptation of the *Spiritual Exercises* of Ignatius Loyola.

For a one- to two-day retreat, divide the time into four equal time periods or phases.

Phase One: Thanksgiving and Remembrance

After reading appropriate Scripture, reflect on it and list the evidences of God's goodness. Recall the circumstances of your conversion and your call to ministry or to the vocation through which you serve God. Enumerate God's blessings to you. *Suggested Scripture:* Psalms 28; 63; 84; Romans 8:28–39.

Phase Two: Knowing Yourself

Acknowledge who you are before God. Be honest and open. Clear a path between yourself and God so that he can show you matters concerning yourself that he wants you to see.

Reflect on the joys and sorrows of recent days and weeks; seek evidence of the Spirit's work in your life and his call to growth and maturity. Enumerate these, confessing sin and shortcomings, acknowledging God's grace where there have been strength, perseverance, and joy. *Suggested Scripture:* Matthew 5—7; Ephesians 4:17—5:21; Colossians 3.

Phase Three: Knowing Christ

Seek to know Christ more fully so that you love him more deeply and serve him more eagerly and effectively. Be drawn to Christ as he is revealed through Scripture. If there is a word of guidance or direction to be received, it will likely come during this phase. *Suggested Scripture:* John 6:1–14, 16–24; 11:17–44; Philippians 2:1–11; Hebrews 4:14–16.

Phase Four: Following Christ

Hear again the word of Christ to be his disciple and servant; reflect on the unique circumstances of that call in response to the retreat; make a fresh commitment to be faithful to that call and to your identity in Christ. *Suggested Scripture:* John 13:1–17; 15:7–17; 2 Corinthians 5:16—6:2; Philippians 3:7—4:1.

APPENDIX 3

Discovering Your Vocation

Recognizing your vocation is as much a process of self-discovery as of discerning God's will. God's call is not arbitrary; it reflects your *dreams* and your *abilities*. Consequently, part of vocational discovery arises from self-knowledge.

In chapter 12 of Paul's letter to the Romans, the apostle enumerates seven gifts by which men and women contribute to the life of the church and to the world. It has been suggested that they are best understood as motivational gifts, as contributions we make that reflect our deep desires and our God-given abilities. Seven are listed: (1) prophesying, (2) serving, (3) teaching, (4) encouraging, (5) contributing to the needs of others, (6) being a leader, and (7) showing mercy. If these are motivational gifts, it is fair to conclude that each person will have only one and will function best in terms of this gift or call. Therefore, part of self-discovery is a recognition of this motivational gift.

Various forms and tests have been designed to help Christians discover the motivational gift, but I have found it helpful to describe and think in terms of a potential ministry setting.

You can ask yourself, How has God gifted me? Where do I see and feel the deep needs of humanity? But consider focusing your attention on a possible crisis scene. Imagine you have entered the emergency room of a hospital and discovered that the patients are lying everywhere, that the lone nurse is off to the side enjoying a cigarette, there are no doctors in sight, the walls are unpainted, and the wounded are weeping in pain.

What do you do? My suggestion is that people will respond in seven classic ways that correspond to the seven motivational gifts.

One fellow recognizes immediately that the problem is that the doctors and nurses *will* not do their responsibilities. They know what is right, and they have the means to fulfill their duties, but they need someone to call them to accountability. This person sees his role as that of calling people to an encounter with the truth. His gift is prophesying.

Others have heard enough preaching and teaching and feel the need of the hour is action—men and women who will get involved with their hands and energies. They are hands-on people, who see what needs to be done and get out and do it. They have the gift of service.

Another sees the main problem to be that the nurses and the doctors do not understand their responsibilities—what is needed is careful explanation. This person is convinced that things will be better when people understand the truth. Her contribution is that of teaching.

Still others look at the situation as lacking hope: What is needed is a restoration of that hope. They suspect the hospital is so run-down because the nurses and the doctors are discouraged. These people bring encouragement. Some are encouragers through their words; others encourage by providing environments of beauty and peace that sustain hope and courage.

Another might look at the situation and decide immediately that what is needed is funding: *Nothing can be accomplished without money, and I know how to raise it.* The person is not coldhearted; it's merely that the gift is that of contributing to the needs of others.

But another might look at the situation and recognize at once that the main problem is organization. What is needed is a person to serve as a catalyst and provide quality administration—to recruit doctors and nurses, and to assure that the proper equipment and supplies are available so that they can do their work. A leader is effective to the extent that the person governs diligently as a servant, freeing others to perform their ministries.

The encourager focuses on the doctors and the nurses. The one who serves immediately gets about the task of tending to the wounded. But there is another whose principal contribution is that of going to the wounded and holding them, carrying their burdens and pains. The person shows mercy and does so with cheer.

Which of the seven is most important? None. If you look closely, you soon see that all seven are a composite picture of the Messiah, the Lord Jesus. He is all seven of these to the church and the world; he works through you to fulfill his ministry as you exercise one of these motivational gifts.

Recognizing your gift does not answer immediately the vocational question, but it is the first step in reflecting on where you can make your maximum contribution. It can help you make a sober-minded choice when two options are before you and one is clearly not a reflection of your dreams and abilities.

APPENDIX 4

Devotional Classics for Spiritual Reading

A. Recommended for All Readers

Augustine, St. *Confessions*.

Bonhoeffer, Dietrich. *Life Together* and *The Cost of Discipleship*.

Merton, Thomas. *New Seeds of Contemplation*.

Thomas à Kempis. *The Imitation of Christ*.

Tozer, A. W. *Knowledge of the Holy*, *The Divine Conquest*, and *The Pursuit of God*.

B. Also Worth Reading

Donne, John. *Devotions*.

Eckhart, Meister. *Talks of Instruction*.

John of the Cross. *Ascent of Mt. Carmel* and *Dark Night*.

Kelly, Thomas. *A Testament of Devotion*.

Law, William. *A Serious Call to a Devout and Holy Life*.

Loyola, Ignatius. *Spiritual Exercises*.

Pascal, Blaise. *Pensées*.

Teresa of Avila. *Interior Castle*.

This is not an exhaustive list. It is selective of different traditions and styles, a place to begin. The works listed under "B" may require more patience, care, and discernment to appreciate their message.

Reading devotional classics requires an approach that is different from the other kinds of reading we do. These suggestions may be useful:

- Read at a time of the day when you are mentally alert.
- Find a time each week, possibly Sunday afternoon after a siesta, to read for an hour or two.
- Refuse to read anything just once. Read each paragraph or section at least twice—if not more often.
- Use a pencil and mark where you have questions unresolved; note where you concur and find encouragement from the author, and also where you are troubled or challenged (you may wish to use a code system to mark the text).
- Conclude with some annotations in a journal or notebook, identifying what you are learning and where the Lord is calling for growth.

NOTES

Chapter One

1. Some notable recent works that are well worth reading are Donald Bloesch, *The Crisis of Piety* (Grand Rapids: Eerdmans, 1968), and *The Struggle of Prayer* (San Francisco: Harper and Row, 1980); David J. Bosch, *A Spirituality of the Road* (Scottdale: Herald, 1979); Richard J. Foster, *Celebration of Discipline* (San Francisco: Harper and Row, 1978); and Richard F. Lovelace, *Dynamics of Spiritual Life* (Downers Grove: Inter-Varsity, 1979).

2. This approach to viewing the church's spiritual history was suggested to me by Professor James Houston's lectures on the history of spirituality in July 1982 at Regent College, Vancouver, Canada.

3. Thomas M. Gannon and George W. Traub, *The Desert and the City* (Chicago: Loyola University Press, 1969).

4. Henry Chadwick, *The Early Church* (Harmondsworth, Eng.: Penguin, 1967), p. 183.

Chapter Two

1. David Keirsey and Marilyn Bates, *Please Understand Me: Character and Personality Types* (Del Mar, Calif.: Gnosology Books, 1984).

2. See Thomas H. Green, S. J., *Come Down Zacchaeus* (Notre Dame: Ave Maria Press, 1987).

Chapter Three

1. Dag Hammarskjöld, *Markings,* translated by Leif Sjöberg and W. H. Auden (New York: Knopf, 1963), p. 147.

2. Thomas Merton, *New Seeds of Contemplation* (London: Burns and Oates, 1961), p. 140.

3. Joseph de Guibert, *Spiritual Doctrine of the Jesuits*, translated by William J. Young, edited by George E. Ganss (Chicago: Institute of Jesuit Sources, 1964), pp. 8–9.

Chapter Four

1. Presented in lectures on the history of spirituality in July 1982 at Regent College, Vancouver, Canada.

2. This threefold paradigm is an adaptation from the *Spiritual Exercises* of Ignatius Loyola, who speaks of knowing, loving, and following Jesus.

Chapter Five

1. Robert E. Webber, *Common Roots: A Call to Evangelical Maturity* (Grand Rapids: Zondervan, 1978).

Chapter Six

1. Kosuke Koyama, *Three Mile an Hour God* (Maryknoll, N.Y.: Orbis, 1979), p. 54.

2. Armando Vallardares, *Against All Hope*, translated by Andrew Hurley (New York: Knopf, 1987).

3. Jeanne Cover, "Theological Reflections: Social Effects of Television," *Religious Education* 78 (Winter 1983): 38–49.

4. Neil Postman, *The Disappearance of Childhood* (New York, Dell, 1982).

Chapter Seven

1. John Carmody, *Reexamining Conscience* (New York: Seabury Press, 1982), p. 30.

2. The term *care-casting* was suggested to me through a sermon delivered by Rev. David Moore in Nyack, New York, in August 1987.

3. Carmody, pp. 3ff.

4. Carmody, pp. 18ff.

Chapter Eight

1. James W. Fowler, *Becoming Adult, Becoming Christian: Adult Development and Christian Faith* (San Francisco: Harper & Row, 1984).

2. Fowler, p. 95.

3. Fowler, pp. 103–4.

4. Fowler, p. 126.

5. Fowler, p. 104.

Chapter Nine

1. David Augsburger, "The Private Lives of Public Leaders," *Christianity Today,* (Nov. 20, 1987), pp. 23–24.

2. Alan Jones, *Exploring Spiritual Direction: An Essay on Christian Friendship* (San Francisco: Harper and Row, 1982), p. 3.

3. Thomas H. Green, S.J., *Come Down Zacchaeus*, p. 95.

4. Jones, p. 19.

Chapter Ten

1. Quoted by James Olthius, *I Pledge You My Troth* (San Francisco: Harper and Row, 1975), p. 107.

2. Olthius, p. 108.

3. Olthius, p. 110.